A House
Divided

A House Divided

Bridging the Generation Gaps in Your Church

Altho written for churches
Smaller than NHUMC
many truths/ideas
for us too.

Bob Whitesel and Kent R. Hunter

Abingdon Press / Nashville

A HOUSE DIVIDED
BRIDGING THE GENERATION GAPS IN YOUR CHURCH

Library-of-Congress Cataloging in Publication Data

Whitesel, Bob.
   A house divided : bridging the generation gap in your church
      Bob Whitesel and Kent R. Hunter.
         p. cm.
   ISBN 0-687-09104-7 (alk. paper)
      1. Church growth. 2. Intergenerational relations—Religious aspects—
Christianity. I. Hunter, Kent R., 1947- II. Title.

BV652.25 .W49 2001
261.8'342—dc21

00-048536

02 03 04 05 06 07 08 09—10 9 8 7 6 5 4 3 2

MANUFACTURED IN THE UNITED STATES OF AMERICA

Contents

Preface

As the church enters a new millennium, warning signs are appearing on the horizon. The Christian church is polarizing along generational lines, and the generation gaps are intensifying this divergence.

In Mark 3:25 Jesus tells us that "if a house is divided against itself, that house cannot stand." This ancient proverb is still relevant today, as generational tensions in our churches separate young people from the maturity and experience that senior members can impart. In addition, the fresh energy and new ideas that younger generations can bring are being forfeited.

As a result of the generation gaps many aging congregations watch their youthful members go elsewhere. Unchurched young people the church desperately seeks to reach with the love and solace of Christ are viewing our churches as irrelevant and inflexible.

The result is that many of these older churches and their proud legacies are doomed to die, if something is not done immediately. A combined consultative experience of over thirty-five years has led us to offer this book as a remedy to this dilemma and as a blueprint for our clients, colleagues, and friends to systematically transform aging congregations into growing tri- generational structures.

This book is written for laypersons, pastors, and denominational leaders who are dealing with intergenerational tensions in their congregations. Our desire is to provide a clear seven-step plan in order to heal—and even benefit from—

the tension between older members of the church leadership and younger generations that are entering our churches and demanding to have input.

In addition, we wish to alleviate the alienation of older members. We believe that, in the name of progress, many of our older members are being pushed aside. Anthropologist Margaret Mead warned, "In most discussions of the generation gap, the alienation of the young is emphasized, while the alienation of the elder may be overlooked. What the commentators forget is that true communication is a dialogue and that both parties to the dialogue lack a vocabulary."[1]

Our desire is to provide a solution and a new vocabulary that retains the historical traditions and liturgy that are so important to our older members, while developing new ministries that reach and assimilate younger generations.

Thus, the tri-generational solution (shortened to Tri-Gen at times), results in a congregation with three generations, peacefully coexisting and stronger due to wider generational appeal. The Tri-Gen model not only offers an alternative to church splits, but also an alternative to the slow death older congregations will experience if they do not have a plan for transferring leadership to successive generations.

It is our firm belief that the Tri-Gen church is one of the best solutions for America's aging congregations, and this book can quickly and directly lead many churches to a healthy and growing multigenerational environment.

Dr. Bob Whitesel
Creative Church Consulting
P.O. Box 788
Winona Lake, IN 46590-0788
www.c3intl.org

Dr. Kent R. Hunter
Church Doctor Ministries
Church Growth Center
P.O. Box 145
Corunna, IN 46730-0145
www.churchdoctor.org

Acknowledgments

I wish to thank my marvelous family for their solace and strength. My lovely wife, Rebecca, remains my best friend, in addition to being my marital partner for twenty-six years. And, I thank God daily for my daughters—Breanna, Kelly, Corrie, and Ashley—who aside from being the joy of this earthly existence, enliven my life with their energy, effervescence, and love.

I also thank my friend, Kent Hunter, for his unselfish support, and for encouraging me to assume the senior editorship of *Strategies for Today's Leader* magazine. I am indebted to the staff and contributing editors of the magazine for their fidelity and devotion to the vision that Donald McGavran birthed more than forty years ago.

I want to thank Fuller Seminary and my theological mentors who helped me see that biblical principles and practical evaluation are colleagues, and not antagonists. I am thankful for Pete Wagner's dry "Aggie" humor, and his ability to make the enigmatic lucid; and to Eddie Gibbs's even dryer English wit and unrivaled methodical approach. I also want to thank George Hunter, for never letting anyone know when he is kidding; Chip Arn, for his willingness to brainstorm; and Gary McIntosh, for being a cherished friend.

I especially want to thank my clients, who constantly assisted in the process of adjusting the strategy and implementation of the Tri-Gen model.

To all of these I owe a deep gratitude. Most of all, I am indebted to my wonderful Lord and Savior, who drew me to himself and gave me more than I ever could expect.

—Bob Whitesel

Continuing where Bob finished, I lift up thanks to Jesus Christ for the amazing privilege he has given us to serve in the marvelous ministry of helping churches. It is an honor to be at the epicenter of the church's need to retool in this twenty-first century.

I marvel at the gifts God has given to Bob Whitesel. He is God's special gift to the church, and a great associate in the cause of "great commission" ministry.

It is with undeniable gratitude that I praise God for my life partner, Janet—a truly remarkable "gift" and for Laura and Jonathan, our two children and best friends. I am grateful for my staff at the Church Growth Center, and for our radio station partners who host The Church Doctor™ program throughout the world. I extend my deep appreciation to my fellow ministry directors: Wayne Register, Roger Miller, Nancy Hines, Jerry Boyers, Paul Griebel, Nels Umble, Greg Ulmer, Brad Benbow, and Jim Manthei. It's an exciting time to be alive and in the ministry of helping churches!

—Kent R. Hunter

Part One

The What and Why
of the Tri-Gen Church

Chapter One

How Generation Gaps Are Tearing Apart Our Churches

*The Needs of America's Churches
Are Changing. Will Our Strategies Adapt?*

The old gentleman looked at me with a countenance that at the same time reflected fear, hope, and dismay. As the rest of the committee drifted in, his expression was mirrored in the voices, uncomfortable stares, and concerned looks of the gathered laity. Now they were pinning their hopes on me, and I felt very uncomfortable in the task. Though this is what I do, I still feel inadequate when undertaking an advisory role with a congregation that is dying.

Slowly, over the past two decades, these church leaders had witnessed a once vibrant congregation of over 350 attendees waste away, due to an aging constituency. Now, faced with a decision to disband the congregation or to hire a consultant for one last attempt to survive, the old gentleman looked at me and asked, "Are we here to bury a friend?"

That night the stress of three similar meetings in three different churches in only six hours was beginning to take its toll. In each meeting, I was cast in the role of advisor and counselor for a congregation that was dwindling. The meeting adjourned, and I found myself retained by another aging congregation worried about its future.

The role and skills of a church growth consultant had

certainly changed over the years. I remember when C. Peter Wagner, one of the founding theorists of the church growth movement, borrowed mathematical metaphors to craft the equations "Celebration + Congregation + Cell = Church"[1] and "Pastor = Leader + Equipper."[2] Such formulas were the primary instruments required in many church growth consultations for years. However, in the latter 1980s the task of equipping churches with the basic formulas of church growth had given way to another more sinister and pressing predicament—churches were declining at an alarming rate due to their inability to attract younger generations.

What is happening? Why are church growth consultants inundated with requests from older congregations desperately seeking to reach out to younger people? And what are the dynamics involved that have led to such a desperate situation?

The authors, two church consultants with a combined experience of 35 years in field research, believe that the ability of the aging church to reach out successfully to younger generations is being hampered by two factors: first, there is a lack of understanding about the emotional intersection where the generations meet. Second, there is a critical need for a clear, workable strategy that will build a healthy "trigenerational church" where three generations peacefully coexist under one roof, one leadership team, and one church name.

Why 85 Percent of Our Churches Are Declining

The Generations Born After 1945 Are Massive and They Are Unchurched

It has been estimated by some researchers that as many as 85 percent of the congregations in America are declining in size.[3] This fact is even more startling when it is recognized that this decline has taken place in the midst of unprecedented population growth. The U.S. Bureau of the Census reports that while there are 83.2 million people living in America who were born in 1945 or before, there are a massive 165.7 million people who have been born since.[4] Figure 1.1 reveals how these latter generations profoundly dwarf their elders.

Figure 1.1 A Comparison of Generations Born Before and After 1945

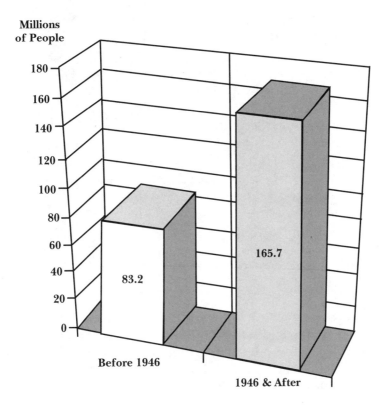

In addition, when compared with those born in 1945 or before,[5] the post–World War II generations are comprised of almost twice as many unchurched people (figure 1.2).[6]

Figure 1.2 Unchurched People in Millions

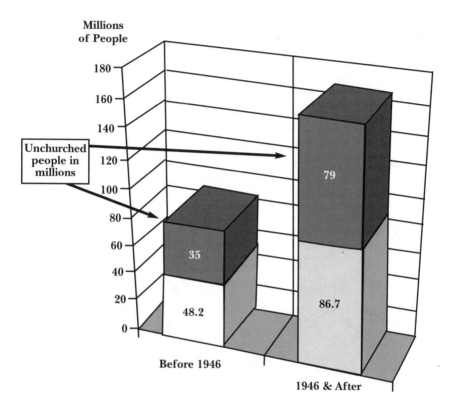

Further complicating the situation is the disturbing trend among younger generations to discontinue church attendance. A nationwide survey reported that church attendance is not only dropping, but is at its lowest ebb in over a decade. Researchers attribute this decline to an increasing abandonment of traditional churches by the disillusioned post–1945 generations.[7]

When this scenario is combined with the prediction that older generations who pay most of the church's bills will be gone in two decades, it becomes clear that the church is facing a crisis of aging. The primary cause of this decline is the church's failure to assimilate younger generations to the same high degree it has successfully incorporated older generations.

Sometimes congregations and even denominations may feel modestly content to ignore such warnings if they have either maintained membership levels or suffered only slight declines in recent decades. However, if these levels are not adjusted for a growing U.S. population, a deceptive presumption of stability will emerge. For example, membership in the Episcopal Church, the Presbyterian Church (USA), the United Church of Christ, and the United Methodist Church has remained relatively steady over the past 30 years. However, when the increasing U.S. population is factored in, it reveals their denominational memberships as percentages of the total U.S. population have all suffered a staggering 45 to 50 percent decline.[8]

Why Young People Avoid First Church

Why don't these massive and predominantly unchurched generations attend aging congregations? It is evident older congregations desperately need a youthful influx. A true story about First Church (a pseudonym) may throw some light on the social and generational dynamics involved.

The battle lines were drawn. A bright, young, single woman had joined First Church eight years before. Early on, she had labored in volunteer tasks often relegated to newcomers: nursery, kitchen duties, and cleaning the church. When several older members at First Church cut back their rigorous volunteer duties, new volunteer openings developed. Her pastor had recently suggested the congregation discover its spiritual gifts through a "Five-Step" process popularized by Peter Wagner.[9] Step Two of this process involved "experimenting with as many gifts as you can." Sensing an opportunity to experiment with her gifts, she volunteered for an opening to teach adult Sunday school.

The class was comprised of many long-standing members

of First Church, several of whom could trace their family heritage in the church to the mid-1800s. All looked forward to the energy and vitality this new teacher would provide. Soon, all agreed she was a gifted and enthusiastic teacher. Many class dropouts returned to share in the excitement. A significant number of the woman's friends began to attend, as well. When the woman noticed a progressive vacuum in the leadership brought on by the rising age of the congregation, she began to actively recruit her friends for leadership positions.

Before long, the church had a burgeoning population of attendees twenty years younger than many long-standing members. The young woman's class became the hub of this youthful influx. Regrettably, the initial enthusiasm of older members began to wane as they saw their class, as well as the church, begin to change in character. Long-standing traditions were left by the wayside, as youthful attendees sought to forge a more contemporary entity out of this dying congregation. Young members saw their influx as the deliverance of the church. Older members saw the influx as a dilution of the principles and practices that had been the historical fountainhead of this congregation's character.

Slowly, the older generation at First Church began to feel their way of congregational life was in jeopardy. A church meeting was the forum for these simmering emotions to overflow. Battle lines were drawn. From older members came variations of, "We've never done it that way before!" In addition, they voiced legitimate concerns that the practices that for years had enhanced their worship experience were now in jeopardy of being replaced by methods foreign to them. Finally, a cathartic outburst exploded with challenges that, "If they [the younger generations] want to do things that way then they should go somewhere else to do it."

The statement pierced the young members of the congregation deeply. They felt they had selflessly jumped into ministry positions in order to help an aging church that was facing dwindling resources. Though they had been members only a short time, they felt that their investment of time, talents, and treasure had led them to view the church as their own. Any thought of leaving would now include the unwelcome prospect of rending relationships and discarding meaningful achievements. Furthermore, the insinuation that they were still second-class latecomers seemed to them to imply that they would never attain the same status that the older members enjoyed, and for which the newcomers secretly longed.

Within three months, most of the younger group was gone. The church's recent growth was now replaced by a deepening downturn in attendance. Not only had the youthful generations left; many older members soon became inactive, sensing an impasse in the church's objectives. Previously, First Church had witnessed a number of younger families passing through the church on an annual basis. Now, the flow seemed to dry up completely. "It's like there is an invisible wall around us," remarked one lay leader. "Word seems to have gotten around about how we treat young families." Her candor surprised me. I wondered why this understanding had not surfaced before First Church had divided along generational lines.

Many people have experienced or heard about similar stories. Part of the reason younger generations learned to avoid First Church was because of the proliferation of such tales. Although perhaps not accurate in detail, they were often rooted in fact. Consequently, prospective younger members became skeptical and pessimistic about their opportunities for leadership and acceptance at First Church.

Younger generations will continue to avoid First Church if the following factors are present.

- Younger generations will avoid a church that makes them feel second class because they do not possess a long history with the congregation.
- A church will not assimilate younger generations if it does not open leadership positions to new members. Younger members will not attain goal-ownership if they

19

are frozen out of the planning and decision-making process. Many of these younger people are climbing the vocational ladder and are accustomed to increasing leadership responsibility in the marketplace.

- Younger generations will avoid a church that primarily offers programs and ministries geared to another generation.

In addition, First Church will feel threatened by an influx of younger members due to the following reasons.

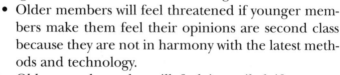

- Older members will feel threatened if younger members make them feel their opinions are second class because they are not in harmony with the latest methods and technology.
- Older members also will feel imperiled if younger members make them feel that the traditions and procedures that mean so much to them are old-fashioned, and therefore are in danger of being eliminated.

Why are so many churches dying when the dilemma appears so obvious and indisputable? Unfortunately, these observations and appropriate corrective measures are clouded by an emotionally charged atmosphere seething in the "generation gaps."

The Emotional Cauldron Where Generations Intersect

If ever there were a cauldron brewing with misunderstanding, disparate perspectives, and distortion, it is the emotional intersection called "the generation gap." Popularized by anthropologist Margaret Mead,[10] the term "generation gap" traditionally defines the chasm that separates the ideals and aspirations of the generation born before January 1, 1946 and those born afterward. The pre-1946 generation is often designated the "Builder Generation" due to a propensity to "build" its world into a social, economic, and military power. They are those born between 1927 and 1945.

Using nineteen-year increments favored by sociologists, it becomes necessary to designate the generation born before 1927 as the" Senior Generation"—the oldest living generation. However, because this Senior Generation mirrors closely the attitudes and perspectives of the Builders, and because their influence is waning, they often are integrated with the Builders into a single generational unit called the Builder Generation. Therefore, for clarity and consistency, the authors have employed the term "Builder" when speaking about the Builder and Senior generations.

The generation gap historically exists between these pre-1946 generations and their offspring: the Baby Boomers. Boomers are so designated because of an upswing in births that followed the returning GIs at the close of World War II. The expression "boom" was appropriated by media pundits to describe this increase in births in the same way a "boom town" in Old West parlance described a town artificially increasing in size due to the discovery of gold or silver. Baby Boomers were born between 1946 and 1964.

Commonly accepted nineteen-year generational spans necessitate another generation be specified from 1965 to 1983. A slight waning of births in 1965 gave rise to the term "Baby Busters." "Bust" was again borrowed from Old West imagery, describing a town that suddenly decreased in size, when the gold or silver ran out, being retermed a "bust" town. Though this generation experienced a decline in births, the term "bust" was clearly a misnomer (as can be seen from figure 1.3). Eventually Baby Buster was replaced by the term "Generation X," designed to portray a nihilistic bent. However, we shall see in chapter 3 that this nihilistic designation is likewise incorrect.

Generation X may not be as numerous as their progenitors, the Boomers, who number 31.7 percent of America, but figure 1.3 demonstrates that it still represents a significant 27.3 percent of the total populace.[11] Generation X is, in fact, the second largest generation America has ever produced, exceeding the national population of all but eleven nations on earth.[12]

Figure 1.3 Generational Ratios

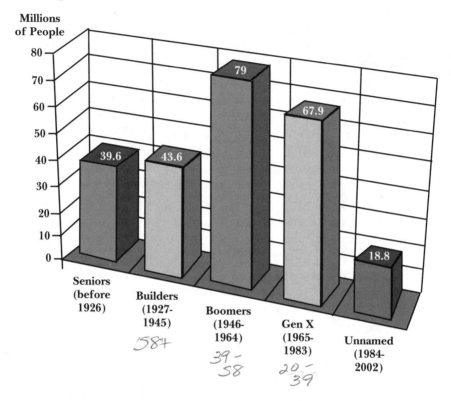

Millions of People

Seniors (before 1926)
Builders (1927-1945) /58+
Boomers (1946-1964) 39 - 58
Gen X (1965-1983) 20 - 39
Unnamed (1984-2002)

Birth Years	Before 1926	1927-1945	1946-1964	1965-1983	1984-2002
Name	Seniors	Buiders	Boomers	Gen X	Gen Y or ?
Millions of People	39.6	43.6	79	67.9	18.8
% of Population	15.9%	17.5%	31.7%	27.3%	7.6%

The maturing of Generation X has led to a second "generation gap" between them and their Boomer parents. Therefore, the authors have pluralized "gap" to "gaps" in this book. This latter generation gap is not perceived to be as large as the gap that separates the Boomers and the Builders. This is, in part, because the Boomers look toward youth for inspiration. This is evident in the way advertisers use youthful imagery to sell products to the Boomers. While the Builders looked to their parents, the Seniors, for inspiration, the Boomer looks to a youth culture for fashion, trends, and artistic expression. The result is that the gap between Generation X and the Boomers is artificially small, due to a Boomer tendency to idolize members of Generation X, perhaps seeing in them a reflection of their idealized selves.

However, Generation X has no such motivation, largely regarding the Boomers as too driven by vanity, opulence, and success. Thus, what gap exists between the Boomer and X generations is largely the creation of Generation X, something that causes great discomfort for the Boomer. We will explore each generation's view across these gaps more thoroughly in chapter 2.

The Battle Lines Are Drawn, But They Are Not Generally Understood

Though the generational battle lines may have been clearly drawn for sociologists, they have only recently begun to be studied by pastors and church leaders. However, the survival of most aging churches, especially those with under 400 attendees, hinges on an understanding of the following generational principles:

The Builder Generation Has a Fear of Being Forced Out by Boomer and Generation X Interests

Together, Generation X and the Boomers make a formidable force. Both populations dwarf the Builders. Though the generation gap often colors the perspective that each generation has of the other, because of their sheer size, the Gen-Xers and Boomers have a potential to paint with a broader brush. Aging churches may feel that if Boomers and Generation X are welcomed unreservedly, they will soon dominate a congregation, relegating the Builder generation to little or no influence. In a worst case scenario, the Builders may even be forced out.

The Boomer Generation Is Expecting to Wield the Same Power in the Church It Has Been Given in the Marketplace

The Boomer generation matured in an environment acquainted with success. Though they were primarily enjoying the fruit of the Builder Generation's labor, Boomers came of age in an era of unheralded prosperity and security. As a result, Boomers may have unrealistic expectations of themselves and others. Yet their optimism, creativity, and sincerity have brought them success in the marketplace. They place great expectations on the church and yearn to participate in its leadership to the same high degree they do in their professions. They are emerging as partners in law firms, captains of industry, creators of new management strategies, and skilled laborers sought for their insights. They will not be content to let others make decisions for them. They have come to expect a significant role in the decision-making process and will avoid any church which makes them feel their advice is unwanted.

Generation X Does Not Want to Be a Clone of the Boomer Generation

Generation X is out to forge its own identity, and many of the idiosyncrasies of the Boomer Generation are distasteful to it. Generation X is interested in establishing institutions that are more tolerant and equitable than those of its successors. Demographer George Barna warns that "Busters are

24

not a generation that is willing to roll over and play dead, allowing the Boomers to call the shots. Busters, in a very different way, are seeking to redesign their environment to create a world which reflects their values, attitudes and dream —within the next 10 to 15 years, there will be a showdown between the numerous, wealthy, cunning Boomers and their reflective, combative successors, the Busters."[13]

A Strategy to Bridge the Gaps

In light of the generational chasms, it becomes clear that the emotional cauldron where the generations intersect can only be bridged by a strategy that:

(1) Begins with a genuine respect for different generational viewpoints

(2) Accepts that different traditions and methodology will be employed by each generation

(3) Understands that there is strength and balance in the generational diversity of a "Tri-generational church"

(4) Realizes that these intergenerational tensions will require the creation of new terminology to delicately handle any potential discord

(5) And accepts the fact that a tri-generational strategy is often the only way an aging church with under 400 attendees can survive

The Church as a Three-Tiered Structure

To understand the strategy that will bridge the generation gaps, we must first understand the typical congregation as a compilation of three groups, each differing in size and each possessing unique strengths. Peter Wagner identified a healthy church as one possessing a three-tier infrastructure of Celebration, Congregation and Cell.[14] Eddie Gibbs borrowed sociological terminology to describe this structure as Primary, Secondary, and Tertiary groups.[15] Many pastors find it easier to think of the three groups in terms of Congregation, Sub-congregation and Cell.

Therefore, for clarity the following terminology is used in the tri-generational approach:

Congregation. This is a Tertiary Group (Gibbs) sometimes called a Celebration Group (Wagner) and usually incorporates 175+ people. It is event oriented, and is characterized by community, identity, and celebration. Another popular designation is the Membership Circle (Schaller[16]).

Sub-Congregation. This is a Secondary Group (Gibbs) sometimes called a Congregation Group (Wagner, Richards[17]), and usually includes 13–175 people. It has a fellowship and task orientation that is characterized by social activity and individual contribution. In addition, it has an environment in which everyone is supposed to know everyone else. The proliferation of secondary groupings is crucial in the multi-generational model. Eddie Gibbs reminds us that "secondary groupings are important for church growth, as they cater to a variety of church-based activities for particular age groups."[18]

Cell. This is a Primary Group (Gibbs), sometimes called a Cell Group (Wagner), and usually includes 3–12 people. It is people centered and is characterized by intimacy and interpersonal involvement.[19] Other popular names include Kinship Circles (Wagner[20]), Face-to-Face Group (Schaller[21]) or Inner Fellowship Circle (Schaller[22]).

Figure 1.4 demonstrates how we will graphically identify the Congregation, Sub-congregations, and Cells in the tri-generational model.

Figure 1.4 The Three Groups Found in a Church

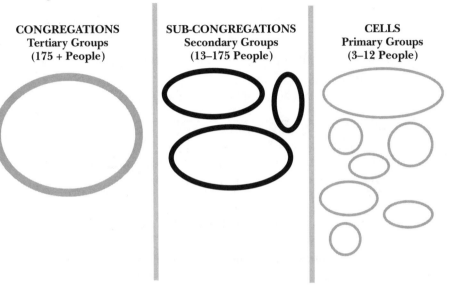

CONGREGATIONS
Tertiary Groups
(175 + People)

SUB-CONGREGATIONS
Secondary Groups
(13–175 People)

CELLS
Primary Groups
(3–12 People)

Figure 1.5 demonstrates how a typical congregation is comprised of what George Hunter calls "a congregation of congregations,"[23] while at the same time has at its heart a web of small cells.

Figure 1.5 How Churches Are Comprised of Three Groups

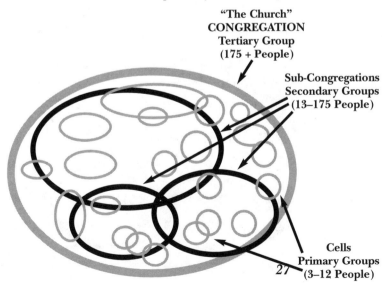

"The Church"
CONGREGATION
Tertiary Group
(175 + People)

Sub-Congregations
Secondary Groups
(13–175 People)

Cells
Primary Groups
(3–12 People)

27

What Is the Definition of a Tri-Gen Church?

We have coined the term "Tri-generational Church" (shortened to "Tri-Gen" at times) to describe a congregational model with three distinct generational sub-congregations peacefully coexisting and thriving. Therefore, we define the Tri-generational Church as the following.

Defining the Tri-Gen Church:
The Tri-Generational Church is a holistic congregation with three distinct generational sub-congregations peacefully coexisting under one roof, one name, and one leadership core.

What Does the Tri-Gen Church Look Like?

In this congregational model, a church will develop into three healthy and thriving secondary groups or "sub-congregations" comprised of Generation X, Boomers, and Builders. Therefore, figure 1.6 shows how a tri-generational church might look.

Figure 1.6 How a Tri-Gen Church Is Comprised of Three Groups

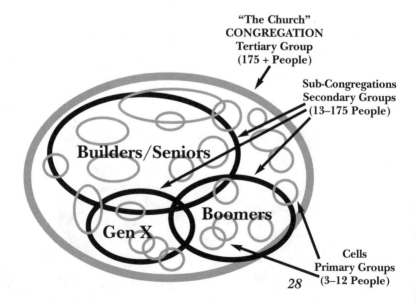

"The Church"
CONGREGATION
Tertiary Group
(175 + People)

Sub-Congregations
Secondary Groups
(13–175 People)

Builders/Seniors

Boomers

Gen X

Cells
Primary Groups
(3–12 People)

28

Figure 1.7: Popular Designations for Congregational Size

Gary McIntosh[24]

Name	Small			Medium	Large
Size	15–200			201–400	401+
Focus	Relational base			Programmatic in orientation	Organizational base

Lyle Schaller[25]

Name	Fellowship	Small	Middle-size	Awkward	Large	Huge
Site	40 or less	50–100	100–175	175–225	225–450	450–700
Focus	Relational base	One big family	It maintains adequate ministries	Doesn't recognize it is a congregation of congregations[25]	It is functioning as a "congregation of congregations."[27]	Administration consumes much time.

For a church of this size to become.............a church of this size, it must become a "congregation of congregation." And this most naturally happens when a church becomes a congregation of generational congregations.

To successfully bridge the generation gaps, a congregation (tertiary group) must possess healthy, sympathetic, and supportive generational sub-congregations (i.e., Generation X, Boomer, and Builder secondary groups). If this interrelated substructure does not harmoniously develop, generational friction will occur, bringing with it a host of damaging consequences.

The Tri-Gen Strategy Helps Small Churches Grow into Medium-Sized Churches

Categorizing churches by size is highly subjective with many competing designations being utilized. Among these, the categories proposed by Lyle E. Schaller have gained the broadest acceptance. However, Gary McIntosh in *One Size Doesn't Fit All* has put forth simpler categories. For in-depth study, Schaller's classifications remain helpful. However, for the sake of clarity and succinctness, the present authors will employ McIntosh's simpler nomenclature. Figure 1.7 compares Schaller's and McIntosh's classifications, as well as depicting how a church's focus changes as growth occurs.

For the small church (200 or fewer attendees), our experience has led us to believe that the tri-generational strategy is usually the only viable option for survival. In today's inflated economy, the church of under 200 will find it a formidable task to fund the level of ministry and number of professional staff expected by today's church-goers. The survival of many small churches depends upon their ability to make the transition from a small-sized church into a congregation of subcongregations (i.e., medium-sized church).

Chapter Two

The Aftermath
of Generational Conflict

Consequences for the Church

They litter the landscape in both rural and urban areas of America. Standing silently, their stained-glass windows and meticulous woodwork are monuments to a Builder generation. Now, they sit in various stages of decay or metamorphosis. Some are homes, others are schools, another might be a daycare facility or theater, but many just sit vacant, monolithic testaments to a dying species. The hallowed caverns that once provided shelter and identity to a Christian community, now exhibit the final stages of an often terminal ecclesiastical affliction sometimes called "Congregational Old Age."

New Models Demand New Terminology

The malady "Old Age" was coined by Peter Wagner to describe an illness that affects a church when residents of the community are leaving and there is little influx into that community.[1] Wagner viewed this as the result of changing community conditions beyond the control of church leadership. He advocated a compassionate pastoral ministry leading to a natural death. This solution might be required in a rural town or village where residents are leaving the farm to live in the city.

However, Wagner was careful to note that old age was not the same as a congregation with an advanced age level.[2] This latter malady is sometimes called "congregational old age" but a closeness to Wagner's wording may at times lead to mislabeling. Therefore, we have chosen to introduce the term "geriatrophy," a combination of the word geriatric, meaning the branch of medicine that deals with the diseases of old age, and atrophy, denoting a wasting away or failure to grow. Geriatrophy, therefore, will distinguish this deadly congregational illness more clearly from ordinary "old age."

While old age may be beyond the control of church members and leaders, geriatrophy can be successfully treated if the community has retained a portion of its younger generations. This is the case in many urban areas and inner suburbs where Boomers and Generation X are moving in search of affordable housing. Recent trends of young people back into rural districts means that even in these communities the potential exists to reverse the effects of geriatrophy.

Another church illness, "ethnikitis," is customarily regarded as the primary killer of churches in America.[3] It is usually narrowly defined as a change in the ethnic culture of a community.[4] However, the word "ethnikitis" is derived from the Greek word *ethne* which means a "people group." Donald McGavran, in his magnum opus on church growth, *Understanding Church Growth*, defined *ethne* as "the classes, tribes, lineages, and peoples of the earth."[5] And Peter Wagner points out that the Strategy Working Group of the Lausanne Committee for World Evangelism defines *ethne* as "a significantly large sociological grouping of individuals who perceive themselves to have a common affinity for one another."[6] As such it can be seen that "ethnikitis" can take on a much broader meaning. A people group could apply equally to Generation X, Boomers, or Builders in addition to those groups distinguished by racial, tribal, or class differences. Therefore, "ethnikitis" might be better identified as a generic term for a host of diseases, as "cancer" is a generic term for a collection of disorders. "Cultural ethnikitis" and "tribal ethnikitis" would thus be two "strains" of the general category "ethnikitis," and "geriatrophy" would be another.

While "cultural ethnikitis" may indeed be a significant killer of churches, several factors lead the authors to believe that "geriatrophy" may have replaced it in this dubious honor. Cultural ethnikitis may be less injurious to congregational health today because:

- Church members are more likely to travel greater distances to a church; hence, a congregation may not be severely handicapped if it remains in its historical location.
- Neighborhood distinctiveness has disappeared in many communities, allowing people to feel comfortable worshiping outside of their residential community.
- Many congregations suffering from cultural ethnikitis have discovered the value of sharing their space with a congregation of different ethnic culture.

Today geriatrophy may be the chief killer of churches in America because of the inability of many congregations successfully to reach across the generation gaps to youthful generations. It is this problem that propels the demand for church consultants as well as books on the issue. At a recent meeting in Chicago, writers and editors affiliated with the American Society for Church Growth agreed that the inability of aging congregations to reach younger generations will be one of the greatest challenges facing the church over the next two decades.

The Dying Church

"I worked all of these years waiting for the day I would retire from the factory and my church duties," a worshiper was overheard to say as he left a church that was dying due to geriatrophy. "Now everyone in our church is retired except for a few people," he continued, "and the church still expects me to do all of my (volunteer) jobs. I'm tired, frustrated, and disappointed. We could plan for retirement from our jobs, why couldn't we plan for retirement at church, too?" When geriatrophy goes untreated, a depressive effect will usually afflict church members.

All too often, the loyal congregants who staffed and maintained church ministries are facing the onset of geriatrophy with limited energy and limited resources. Most retired persons live on fixed incomes. The increase in income that churches enjoyed as their members climbed the employment ladder will plateau as their members retire. Yet, the costs of repairing and maintaining aging buildings continue to rise.

Retired church members often envision a day when they may rest from the busyness of their good works, as another generation takes up the reins of leadership. Yet, too often the days to reach out to the younger generations pass them by before they are aware of the quandary they face.

At one time or another in most churches, there has been a viable primary (cell) or secondary group (sub-congregation) comprised of a younger generation. However, due to inadvertent feelings of second-class stature or an inability to penetrate the leadership structure, these youthful cells or sub-congregations may have slowly dissipated. Usually, members of such a group will discover another congregation more open to their influx, disengage from their commitments in the aging church, and move elsewhere (figure 2.1). The process is usually not formally organized, but is only an unofficial exodus. But when the aging congregation discovers what is happening, it usually is too late to stem the tide.

At other times, a youthful pastor will be hired in hopes that he or she will successfully reach the younger generations. Unfortunately, too often this pastor is designated the primary visionary and worker in the process. The church

Figure 2.1 Church A Is Dying from Geriatrophy

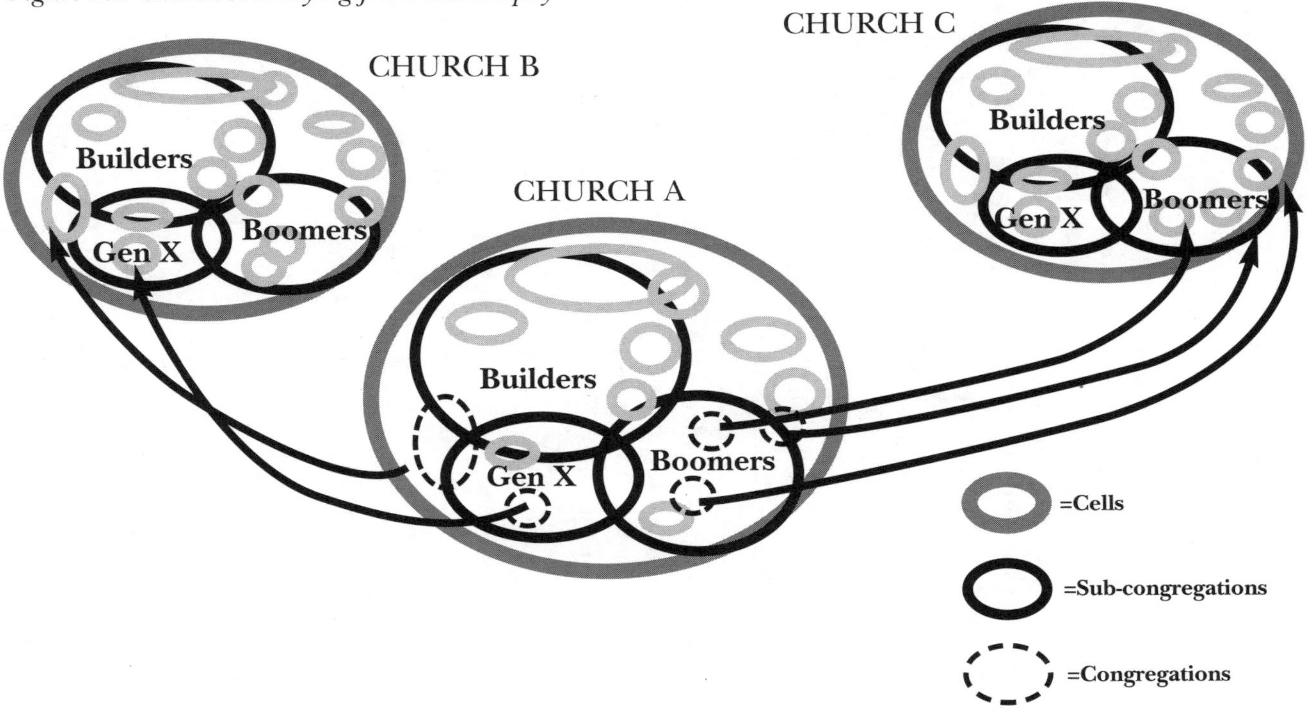
CHURCH B
Builders
Gen X
Boomers
CHURCH A
Builders
Gen X
Boomers
CHURCH C
Builders
Gen X
Boomers
=Cells
=Sub-congregations
=Congregations

leadership is often unaware of the challenges and changes that will be required to reach out successfully to younger generations. When the new pastor tries to implement the changes needed to reach the younger generations, he or she may be forced out due to failure to provide a demonstrable rationale for such venturesome changes. The church leadership may feel the pastor does not possess a clear and concise plan that will reach out to the younger generations, while protecting the traditions and practices that mean so much to the older generations.

Without a clear and proven plan, many congregations will face one of two destinies. Either they will die a slow and agonizing death, or they will suffer a generational upheaval—comparable to an earthquake where the landmasses separate—resulting in a generational fissure that defies bridge building across the ensuing chasm.

The Builder generation, which takes such pride in the fruit of its labor, often faces the distasteful option of selling a building they have lovingly maintained for many years. "This building and its people are the last thing I have," remarked one woman. "My husband is gone, and I don't think I can bear having someone take my church from me." She motioned for me to follow and led me down the stairs to a small fellowship hall in the basement. "This room was named for my husband. Who is going to remember?"

The Unplanned Offspring

A beautiful octagonal sanctuary rises from a Midwestern cornfield. The church buildings are laid out in a horseshoe design, embracing a large, spacious parking lot. This congregation takes pride in the fact that the facilities are well kept, although all of its work, including all pastoral tasks, is accomplished by volunteers. The congregation is an exciting mixture of Boomers and Generation X with blue collar and farming backgrounds.

In contrast to the modernness of this church sits the mother church, less than two miles away. Nestled among mature maple trees on the edge of a small farming community, the stately brick structure houses a dwindling congregation of Builders. In small town America, it is not polite to air one's dirty laundry publicly; thus few will discuss the generational conflicts that led the younger members to establish their own congregation some ten years earlier.

A bit of sleuthing uncovers that the cause was generational tension, similar to that discussed earlier in this chapter, but the outcome was different. In this situation, the sub-congregation of Boomers left intact from the mother congregation to found their own nearby congregation. Though the split was bitter and many sharp words were privately exchanged, publicly both generations lauded the decision. Nevertheless, many relationships were damaged with emotional lacerations that take years to heal in small town America. "I can't drive by without feeling sorry for those people," remarked the young mother and a member of the unplanned offspring. "Some of those people were like grandparents to me. I wonder if they ever forgave us."

This is an all too typical aftermath of generational conflict, the unplanned offspring. In this scenario, as the mother church ages, a significant Generation X and/or Boomer generation leaves to found a younger church nearby (figure 2.2). This course may make it harder than ever for the aging congregation to develop another secondary Generation X and/or Boomer generation, since the nearby church provides a ready-made alternative for the younger generations. Yet, without corrective action, the mother church is heading toward difficult times with an aging constituency. Depending on the quality of the relationship the mother church maintains with its offspring, the mother church may expect little to no help wrestling with the problems of geriatrophy.

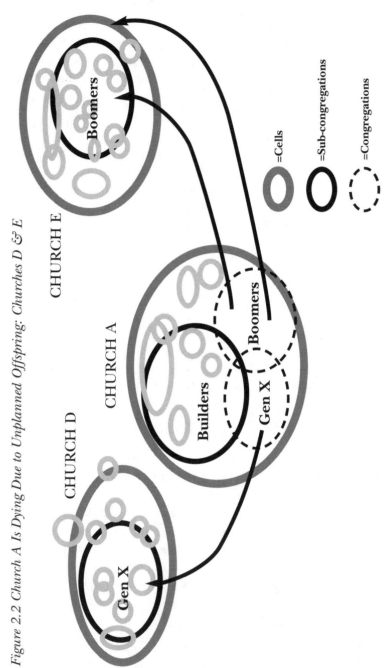

Figure 2.2 Church A Is Dying Due to Unplanned Offspring: Churches D & E

CHURCH D

CHURCH A

CHURCH E

Gen X

Builders

Boomers

Gen X

Boomers

◯ =Cells

⬭ =Sub-congregations

◌ =Congregations

The Unstable Boomer Congregation

"We have never come to grips with our history, and that's why we are repeating it." The young Wisconsin pastor sat across the desk from me with an uncompromising and determined look in his eye. We had been discussing the history of the Boomer congregation of which he had recently become pastor. It seemed like the perfect match. The leaders I interviewed were definitely enthusiastic about their new shepherd, and he was one of the most insightful and engaging men I knew. Yet, he recognized from the onset that this thriving Boomer congregation was experiencing difficulty reaching out to the Generation X.

The church had been birthed as an "unplanned off-spring" of a Builder church in town. The name of the mother church was taken from the street on which it was built. Names like "Maple Avenue Church" are often a Builder generation preference that may unconsciously underscore its attachment to a structure. Remember this is not necessarily bad, for when the Builder generation creates a house of worship with stained-glass windows and magnificent woodwork, it is viewed by this generation as a testimony to God-given artistic skill. Religious artistry is a form of worship for many of the Builder generation, an inclination rooted in European heritage where great cathedrals still stand as monuments to centuries of artisan toil.

When the unplanned offspring withdrew from the aging mother church to form its own congregation, they adopted terminology that reflected their Boomer philosophy. The church was called "Community Church," thereby stressing its community rather than its edifice. The motto on the church letterhead, "A church made of people, not buildings," seemed to be a Boomer battle cry and almost a taunt to their former congregation. The new building itself was a contemporary structure, centered around a multipurpose auditorium that could be used for basketball. The outside facade was trimmed in roughhewn wood left to weather naturally and devoid of any hint of stained glass. The church was situated on the far edge of the city's suburbs, and many of the young people moving to the area found the church a delightful and well-suited home.

In this idyllic setting, the pastor saw misfortune on the horizon. The inability of the Boomers to open their leadership structure to Generation X had led to an impediment in reaching the younger generation. Though this congregation appeared stable and secure on the outside, without the development of a Generation X sub-congregation, the church would one day face the same malady the Builder congregation it left now faced—geriatrophy.

The ordeal of an "unplanned offspring" is a woeful experience for a daughter church if the daughter is a Boomer congregation. The Boomer offspring will not have a positive experience in a multigenerational environment. Therefore, the unstable Boomer offspring may be handicapped in its efforts successfully to develop a Gen-X sub-congregation and preserve its future. The pastor probably did not know his statement was mirroring American philosopher George Santayana's observation that, "Those who cannot remember the past are condemned to repeat it."[7]

The Ineffectiveness of the Usual Solutions

The One-Generation Church

My teammate desperately tried to grab the baton, but bedeviled by my competitor, I didn't notice how carelessly I bobbled it. Less than a second later, the baton I had so gingerly tried to pass, bounced down the cinder track. Back in the locker room, my track coach would chasten me with these words: "The transfer of the baton is what separates you from being just another runner. Passing the baton is the most important skill you can acquire. I don't think you're that much of a team player. You are better running on your own." I don't think my coach tried to hurt my feelings, only motivate me to stick with my strengths. But he had driven his lesson home—and he was right. An only child, I always practiced my running skills unaccompanied. I was not very good at working with others, much less skillfully passing a baton.

Every congregation is in a generational relay and must prepare for an eventual passing of the baton of leadership to a successive generation. Those who practice working as a tri-generational team will more easily succeed when the actual passing is required.

Our observation is that the leading reason churches are declining is because most are staffed, programmed, and envisioned to reach one generation. Churches naturally gravitate toward this "one generation" environment, in part because, as Donald McGavran observed in *Understanding Church Growth*, "People like to become Christians without crossing racial, linguistic or class barriers."[8] This is why, when people are visiting a church, they instinctively ask the social question, "Are there people like me here?" If they can answer in the affirmative, they are attracted to that fellowship. These dynamics tend to produce churches where members consider each other to be "our kind of people." This principle has been lauded for its cohesive nature, as well as castigated for its exclusivity.[9]

However, this like-mindedness can unintentionally stunt growth by creating a one-generational church. Yet, all of the social barriers identified by McGavran—racial, linguistic, and class—are primarily age neutral. Boomers who are African American would not feel they have crossed racial barriers by joining a predominantly Builder African American congregation. The same is true of a blue-collar Gen-Xer joining a blue-collar Boomer congregation. Racial and class distinctions are usually transgenerational, so they provide no impediment for the Tri-Gen church. Language, however, can possess a generational bias in its use of idiom and vernacular. However, if the same mother tongue is spoken, language will not usually produce a generational growth barrier.

While generational like-mindedness does propel assimilation, churches do not have the luxury of allowing this to mutate into generational exclusivity. All one-generation churches will eventually die of geriatrophy. The future for such congregations is ill fated. Any redirection toward a trigenerational church will only become harder the longer a congregation delays. One-generation churches will eventually be faced with a challenge of passing the baton of leadership. How skillful will that transfer be? Or, will it even take place?

THE SATELLITE MODEL

Some congregations experiencing intergenerational tension may opt for a "planned offspring" approach where a daughter church is deliberately planted either in the existing building or in a facility nearby. This model seeks to allow younger generations to develop their own congregation independent of the mother church.

Initially this appears to be a prudent course. But, typically, in these situations, the generation gaps intensify because there is little motivation for either generation to pursue teamwork and mutual understanding. Two or more congregations may readily develop, but without a shared decision-making process, the congregations will usually polarize. They may only realize their need for one another after the die is cast.

THE SEEKER MODEL

The Seeker Celebration is a popularized model designed to reach unchurched people with an engaging, relevant, and uplifting experience. Pioneered by Bill Hybels in South Barrington, Illinois, it is best represented by churches of the Willow Creek Association.[10]

Sometimes an aging congregation will embark upon a

seeker-sensitive celebration in hopes of appeasing a growing sub-congregation of Boomers and/or Gen-Xers. However, this remedy is incomplete, ignoring the reality that "celebration" is only one facet of a holistic generational ministry. A balanced growth strategy involves four fundamental "Cs":

- **Cultivate** spiritual growth through teaching ministries
- **Care** for God's people through care giving
- **Communicate** Christ's love through outreach ministry
- **Celebrate** God's goodness through worship

The Four Cs demonstrate that the Seeker-Celebration by itself will fall short in addressing the holistic needs of a generational sub-congregation. Part 2 of this book, "7 Steps to a Tri-generational Church," will present a thorough strategy for simultaneously meeting the four fundamental "Cs" in Builder, Boomer, and X generations.

THE BLENDED MODEL

"It's not fair! I don't like to hear radio music and I shouldn't be forced to listen to it at my church." I didn't expect these words from the lips of a respected and innovative choral director. Though now advanced in years, in the 1950s and 1960s he had organized dozens of tours of Europe for teenage choral groups. His innovative ideas were almost legendary in the community. "I don't mind creativity," he volunteered, "but don't ruin my worship experience. I only get an hour a week with my friends, and you want to spoil it with fifteen minutes of your radio music. No thanks! Radio music goes—or I go!" After forty years of ministry in this congregation, he was soon relieved of his choral position.

While too much separation gives rise to separate entities, too little separation discourages generational identity. The choral director felt deprived of a quarter of his weekly worship experience by the inclusion of contemporary music. Of course, many of the Boomers in his congregation had been pushing for the inclusion of even more of their music.

43

This story demonstrates a serious problem in the often attempted strategy of "blending" elements of each generation's interests and preferences into one entity. According to Gary McIntosh's research, blending two or more differing philosophies of ministry, usually in the same worship experience, results in "continuing tension over the philosophy of ministry."[11] Without diffusing this tension over competing philosophies, generation gaps will persist and often widen. To change programming without addressing underlying philosophical tensions is like treating the symptom without medicating the illness. The Tri-Gen approach replaces these rival philosophies of ministry with a unified philosophy. This approach offers an alternative to the blended model, which often does not satisfy either generation.

"I'm tired of them forcing their ideas on us. Just when I start to worship, they throw in one of their songs and it spoils the whole mood. If they want a worship service like that, they've got plenty of churches that do it that way. Let them go there!" You could cut the tension with a knife that night, and tears could be seen appearing in the corner of the eyes of several members of the worship committee. Two older gentlemen walked out, and another rift was beginning that might take months or perhaps years to heal. Surprisingly the speaker was not a Builder or Boomer, but a member of Generation X who had only joined the church in the last year, and now had entered the philosophical fray firmly on the side of his generation.

The blended model was a noble attempt at a Tri-Gen church, but in many areas it does not go far enough, and in some areas it goes too far, and only accentuates generational gaps.

THE RESTART MODEL

Some denominations have a program in place designed to resurrect an aging congregation. Sometimes called the "restart model" or the "regeneration process," this procedure allows a church to dissolve the present entity and form

44

a new congregation with help from nearby congregations of the same polity. Components of this program usually include the following:

(1) The present church committees are disbanded and a new "steering committee" is appointed. This new committee will be comprised of members of the restart church and neighboring churches of the same denomination. The majority (51+ percent) of this steering committee will be from congregations other than the restart church. This committee will guide the church for one to three years.

(2) The church will usually close for a six-month period of time. During this time, home Bible studies will continue for members of the restart church, in order to provide continuity. This allows a time for mourning of the demise of the former union and introspection on the type of congregation that should emerge.

(3) The church will actively seek a new pastor, and the church will usually not reopen until it has new pastoral leadership in place.

The restart model is a viable alternative to closure and has been employed extensively by the American Baptist churches. While unable to preserve the traditions or history of the aging church, this approach does preserve a denominational presence in the community.

However, the advice below must be considered when considering the restart or regeneration model.

(1) The church leadership must be ready to relinquish control of the new organization to a steering committee comprised of people outside the local congregation

(2) Church members must understand that their spiritual sustenance will come from a small group setting for at least six months during the transition phase.

This model is frequently successful in planting a new and often younger congregation in the same community as the aging church. However, older members of the former congregation usually do not make it through the transition, due to two important reasons.

First, Builders are accustomed to sharing intimacy and closeness through Sunday school classes, which often are their cell groups. Home Bible studies, while more popular among Boomers, do not provide an attractive alternative to Builders, who traditionally have enjoyed small group intimacy through the Sunday school format.

Second, the restart model works best when the existing leadership is fragmented or nonexistent. The restart strategy then provides needed leadership to fill the void. However, if an existing and long-lived leadership is already in place, and in most aging churches this is the case, the restart model often prunes a majority of these steadfast saints from the process. Long-standing leaders will feel they are no longer wanted or needed, and resistance to forward progress often spreads informally among the aging congregation.

Although the restart model is effective in establishing a younger church in the community context, it usually fails in preserving a Builder sub-congregation.

THE CLOSURE MODEL

Closure usually necessitates the dissolution of the legal corporation that comprises the aging church. According to state law, this may require some or all of the following steps: Selling or donating all assets, buildings, and land (and/or the return of such to the denominational association); disbanding of all committees, fellowships, groups, and ministries; and an attempt to fold in individuals of this congregation into other community congregations or affiliated congregations nearby.

As can be seen from the above steps, this is a very arduous direction. Any decision to follow this course must be undertaken carefully and after thorough consideration of all options. Once this course of action is embarked upon, you cannot go back. Much of a church's health is derived from the congregation's "perception" or "image" of itself, so this action usually further injures congregational self-esteem. If the congregation starts in this direction and then decides to change its mind, it will be almost impossible to reverse the momentum. The route to closure is a one-way street.

Closure usually leaves many longtime church members without a church, due to their age and their strong community identity. The Builder generation has a heightened loyalty to its municipality as well as its local church, since both are testimonials to the labor required to build a civil and spiritual society. Thus, Builders will usually not attend a congregation outside of their municipality, nor will they attend another local congregation due to a strong sense of allegiance. Closure, like a restart, usually deprives aging church members of their spiritual identity and Christian community.

THE MERGER MODEL

A merger involves obtaining consent from a nearby congregation to allow a congregation to merge with it. Several factors are required to attain a successful merger.

(1) Mergers are most successful when "equal mergers" are attempted. This means that the congregations are of roughly the same size and the same congregational age.
(2) Mergers are most successful when there is a low amount of community identity.
(3) Mergers are most successful when the churches are within the same community or are in proximity.

Successful mergers will usually require a merger of committees, ministries, and celebrations. This can be clumsy and unpleasant, especially if the following factors are present.

47

(1) If both churches have long histories of members who have been influential in the church's leadership, their involvement may be unceremoniously curtailed.

(2) If one church is larger than the other church, the leadership will not integrate smoothly. The smaller church leadership will be employing different management styles from the larger church. Often these management styles, while necessary for the size of each congregation, are now incompatible and the cause of friction. Mergers of a smaller congregation into a larger congregation will usually result in the loss of identity for the smaller congregation. The history of the smaller church, a "glue" that holds together the Builder generation, will usually be lost.

Due to these challenges, mergers over time usually do not result in any net attendance gain. For example: If the smaller congregation averaged fifty in attendance, and the larger congregation one hundred and fifty in attendance, we might expect a total merged size of two hundred. Yet, after a period of three or more years, the merged congregation will usually have reverted to the pre-merged size of the larger congregation: one hundred and fifty. The net loss to the denomination is fifty.

Problems are compounded if both merged churches are Builder congregations, and usually when the merger option is considered this is the case. A merger of two aging congregations will only slow the rate of decline; it will not correct it. For a short time, they will enjoy a larger organization, but in three to five years, the church will be again facing dwindling numbers. Thus, merger among Builder congregations only forestalls decline. The use of this strategy by an aging church should only be employed when a congregation needs to buy time; for example, to sell a building, undergo a pastoral transition, or strengthen a fiscal position. The by-product of this strategy is also a loss of many aging members who, because of their increasing lack of mobility and heightened loyalties, may not participate in the merger. Thus, the ranks of unchurched believers in the community will frequently increase.

The Tri-generational Model Offers

Immediacy

In the next decade, the lay men and women born before 1946 and who guided many of our prominent churches will reach retirement. As they near this social milestone, many are looking to younger congregants to succeed them in their volunteer responsibilities. However, in many congregations, these younger generations are distressingly absent, and the Builder generation is discovering that the generation gaps are threatening to separate them from an intact legacy.

A Builder generation who pays the majority of our congregational bills will, over the next two decades, fade from our congregations.[12] Prior to this, many retirees will live on fixed or dwindling incomes. When an inflated economy and the uncertain future of governmental assistance are taken into account, it is indisputable that Builder congregations will face intensifying financial instability.

Churches govern by consensus of vision, and therefore can be painfully slow in successfully addressing this predicament. Congregations that have the most success will have a clear plan and commence it at the earliest opportunity.

A "7 Steps to a Tri-generational Church," outlined in detail in part 2 of this book, can be swiftly launched to foster transgenerational longevity. The inevitable consequences of the generation gaps will overtake the aging churches of America, regardless of awareness or preparation. Without a plan, many proud and prominent congregations sit on the precipice of an uncertain future.

Relevancy

John's eyes beamed at me with the joy that comes from holding a twelve-week-old newborn. I had always regarded John as the epitome of smartness and fashion for the upwardly mobile young professional. I had admired John's style and today was no exception: horn-rimmed glasses, power suit, classy tie, and a fashionable haircut. Somehow, it seemed just a little incongruous to see this forty-something business type bouncing a newborn bundled in pink and white. But today, John seemed a million miles away from the fashion slave I knew. Today this bundle of joy preoccupied him entirely.

"Can you tell she's got my hair?" John boasted, pointing to the snippet of golden locks that emerged from the blankets. Then John was off, showing all who might hesitate in the church's foyer the genetic similarities between himself and his offspring. Soon he returned and confided, "I wish I didn't have to leave this morning, but I've got to go. I want my parents to see how glorious their great-granddaughter looks." And, with that announcement, John was out the door, headed to a nearby church where his parents and others of their generation worshiped.

John was a Boomer and a grandfather, an emerging genus in the Boomer species. Later John would confide in me that although his congregation was a large and lively Boomer congregation, his newfound grandfather status reminded him of how much he missed a church with multiple generations. "It seems like we've split the church into competing groups. One old, trying to just keep going. One young, too occupied with church growth and not concerned enough about family." John was one of the leaders of his church and well versed in church growth principles, but only through his journey to grandparenthood had he become aware of the inadequacy of the one-generational environment.

The Tri-Gen model provides the cross-generational bridge that is lacking even in seemingly successful one-generation churches. As Boomers are thrust into the roles of grandparents, they are rediscovering the relational strength of a congregation where grandparents, parents, and children mature in their Christian faith side by side.

The author of the Epistle to Titus reminded a young pastor of the church at Crete that the presence of older women in the congregation was a valuable resource for the younger women. When the older women are diligent to cultivate a reverent behavior (Titus 2:3), they became a sevenfold inspiration to younger women, helping the latter discover how to love their husbands, love their children, be self-controlled, pure, busy at home, kind, and subject to their husbands (Titus 2:4-5).

Regardless of any gender provincialism that may or may not be part of the author's intention, the passage clearly demonstrates that an intergenerational bridge provides vital lessons for a local congregation. And how else could the biblical author expect the church on Crete to follow his advice unless that church possessed a multigenerational environment?

Proficiency

It is true that the continuity of all cultures depends on the living presence of at least three generations. —Margaret Mead[13]

In the same rural farming community where we earlier described the birth of an "unplanned offspring," there sits another congregation with a brighter future. The latter we shall call "The Church of Main Street," and it has embraced the tri-generational model.

"When our aging church was looking for a pastor, I saw they were facing a paradox," deduced the church's Boomer-age pastor. "They wanted someone who was young and possessed the energy to move the church forward, but they also wanted a person whom they could view as a peer. They wouldn't follow a pastor unless they were convinced he understood and appreciated the over-fifty generation. I knew if I was not prepared to employ a strategy that addressed their needs, too, I'd better have my résumé ready." This pastor had anticipated the pragmatic reality of a tri-generational strategy.

The Church on Main Street has emerged as the only growing church in this rural community of a dozen churches by recruiting unchurched Boomers and members of Generation X to join its church family. During this same time, the "unplanned offspring" has plateaued and its "mother church" has declined. The Church on Main Street, on the other hand, has inaugurated two Sunday services. Musing on the reasons for this progress, the pastor noted that the tri-generational strategy had increased the size of the church's potential harvest field. "Let me explain how this happened," continued the minister. "I've heard that when people come to church they are asking the question: 'Are there people like me here?' Because we are consciously ministering to three different generations, chances are they are going to find somebody they can relate to. We can minister to a greater percentage of the community 'and we've grown because of it!' "

By allowing a church to minister to a greater percentage of the community, the tri-generational strategy also increases the probability a local congregation will grow in a transitory society. Donald McGavran is often remembered for his disquieting observation that since America has a very mobile population "we won't keep all we win and consequently we must be continually winning, even to stand still."[14] The tri-generational model overcomes this inertia by allowing the local church to relate to a greater percentage of its neighbors.

The Tri-Gen strategy is proficient in every environment in which it has been tried. Rural, suburban, and urban contexts all provide appropriate settings in which a tri-generational church will flourish. The following societal factors are responsible for the broad applicability of the Tri-Gen model:

Rural. Over the first thirty years of the Church Growth Movement, rural communities were declining, and a considerable amount of ink was penned on how to address this crisis. Most of this focused on the survival of the rural church during an exodus brought on by the demise of the family farm. Those unable to flee this economic misfortune were usually aging residents, who by default became the caretakers of the rural church.

The 1990s witnessed an encouraging trend, as rural communities experienced an influx of upwardly mobile urbanites seeking solace and relief from city life. Demographers for the U.S. Department of Agriculture reported that in the early 1990s, almost two-thirds of the nation's rural communities gained in population.[15] This is in sharp contrast to their findings in the 1980s when more than half of these same communities lost residents. The maturing of the Boomer generation and their eschewing of the city life are cited as the engine that fueled this geographical change.

Church growth has taken a renewed interest in the expanding harvest of souls accessible to the rural church. Many recent books have offered new strategies tailored to the small rural congregation.[16] Rural churches are once again flourishing.

However, inevitable tension has arisen as Boomers reenter rural churches seeking to participate on a level equal to their responsibility in large urban churches. Upon their unexpected return, Boomers have discovered that many Builders and Seniors view them as deserters. The generational chasm has thus widened by the anticipations of the Boomers and the apprehensions of the Builders.

The Tri-Gen strategy is pivotal in such venues, offering Boomers access to leadership opportunities while concurrently alleviating Builder apprehensions.

Inner suburbs. Suburbs, which nestle against the city limits of many urban areas, are also undergoing a renaissance. Cost-conscious Gen-Xers are invading communities that once were the traditional domain of aging Builders. In these inner suburbs, the potential to grow a church comprised of Builder and Generation X sub-congregations is sizable.

Some aging congregations in the inner suburb find it easier to leap across two generation gaps and reach Generation X, while ignoring the Boomers altogether. While this approach may not seize upon the holistic strength of a Tri-Gen model, it does compensate for the limitations of a one-generational church by adopting a bi-generational format. This bi-generational variation provides stability and strength for congregations that are unable to reach Boomers. Establishing a bi-generational church requires only that the "7 Steps to a Tri-generational Church" outlined in part 2 of this book, be applied with two generations rather than the targeted three.

Outer suburbs. The upper middle class has historically developed suburban communities further and further removed from the urban center. This is sometimes referred to as "suburban sprawl." The advent of limited-access highways has made commuting from these areas a viable option for those seeking breathing space and a perceived security. As such, these areas are often the communities of choice for successful young families, many of whom are Gen-Xers and Boomers.

Here again the Tri-Gen model provides the important role of linking upwardly successful Boomers and Generation X with middle-class Builders who first moved to the area when it was still semi-rural.

Urban. Much of the difficulty of living in depressed urban areas revolves around the lack of intact family structures. The tragic absence of men in many homes has put undue pressure and strain on single mothers and their children. The Tri-Gen strategy provides a pivotal intergenerational environment, in which the parenting skills of aging Builders can be shared with young Gen-Xers and Boomers struggling with fragmented family structures.

Some portions of urban areas are also undergoing a remarkable renaissance. In these areas, high-density dwellings have been razed in favor of new townhouse-style accommodations marketed to an emerging middle class. These residents are often Generation X and Boomer families who share with the older residents an appreciation for family, hard work, and community pride. Though urban areas have always accommodated a wide generational mix, the intermingling of three generations has also led to a certain amount of strain. The church, as the traditional "glue" of urban areas, can more readily unify these generations when employing the tri-generational approach.

The ability of the Tri-Gen strategy to bring forth a healthy and holistic transgenerational church can only be understood by first looking at the cultural values of the Gen-X, Boomer, and Builder generations. The following chapter explains the genesis of these generational chasms.

Chapter Three

Attitudes
That Produce the Gaps

Generation X

I Guess We're Called Generation X

She was the model of a church-going teenager. One of only a handful of youth who had remained part of a small young group in her dwindling church. "I don't think the church realizes how hard it is to be the only senior in the youth group. I hardly have any friends at church my age. But next year I'll be at a Christian college and I'll have tons of friends," she predicted. "How does it feel to be a Baby Buster in a Boomer church?" I queried. "Don't call me a buster. What's a buster anyway? I don't know who came up with that word." After a pause she said, "I guess we're called Generation X."

It was Boomers who first began to refer to them as "Generation X" instead of Baby Busters, a name that never really caught on. The "X" was meant to refer to a nihilistic attitude the Boomers thought they noticed across the widening generation gap. However, if a name is imposed by one generation across the generation gap upon another, the result is likely to be an ill-received designation. Even when global marketers such as the Pepsi Cola Company tried to soften the image to "Generation NeXt" the younger generation refused to be converted. But the generation gap often produces a craving to shock and startle the generation on the other side. And so, it is little wonder that the young people shunned the term Buster in favor of the former disparaging name, Generation X.

Busting Our Stereotypes

The refusal of the younger generation to be called Baby Busters is probably a blessing. In chapter 1 we saw that it is not really a "bust" at all. Although 1964 did witness the beginning of a decline in the high birth rate of the Baby Boomers, the "bust" was really not much of a downturn. Remember, Generation X is the second largest generation ever born in America, and it exceeds the national population of all but eleven nations on earth.[1] Clearly, they are not the result of a "bust" in births.

But if Generation X is not really a "bust" generation, it is not really an "X" generation either. Remember, the "X" in the name was given by a Boomer generation gazing across the generation gap, which thought it perceived a nihilistic and rebellious age group. However, when we look more closely at Generation X, we find its members are not all that nihilistic or rebellious. In fact, in many ways, they mirror the values of their parents and even grandparents.

Over a three-year period, researcher George Barna sampled almost fifteen hundred respondents of the Generation X age group. The results burst many of the stereotypes held by Boomers. Barna's research uncovered that the majority of Generation X is involved in some type of church or religious group, and that those in this age group talk with their friends about religion more than their parents do.[2] Among Generation X, a massive 91 percent believe in God or a "higher power," and 66 percent believe there is only one God and that He created the universe. In addition, 62 percent hold that God hears all people's prayers and has the power to answer those prayers; and 50 percent are convinced Jesus Christ is God's Son who arose from the dead and is alive today.[3]

Although Generation X is religious, it has a mixed view about the absoluteness of Christianity. Although 66 percent believe there is only "one God and that He created the universe," this is rather low when compared with a massive 91 percent of Generation X who ·believe in God or a higher power. Generation X appears to have been wooed away from the doctrine of God's supremacy in favor of more inclusive religious beliefs, mainly "new age" or Eastern in spirit. The outcome is that while Generation X is definitely not nihilistic or irreligious, it is definitely underaddressed by the Christian church.

The Personality of Generation X: The MTV Work Environment

On every desk in this trendy Manhattan office complex is a television, issuing a barrage of color, sensuality, melody, and action. Each set is tuned to the same channel, Music Television, more popularly known as MTV. The office is filled with Generation X workers, casually attired in the latest fashionable piercings and apparel. Across America and around the world, images of this part office, part studio are radiated by cable and satellite. To many of those of Generation X, this looks like a business nirvana, the ideal working environment. Though most of the rules in this Gen-X paradise are few and trivial, there is one rule that must not be transgressed. The unbreakable rule is that the television at each desk must always remain on, though muted, if need be. Such unusual stipulations result from the philosophy that these broadcasts are the cultural portal for MTV programmers and journalists who are changing the way Generation X thinks. *The New Yorker* magazine concluded that through this environment "their (MTV) bosses want them to absorb as much of the language and the sensibility of MTV as possible."[4]

Even in middle America, MTV has become the surrogate babysitter for many youth arriving home after school to an empty house. To Generation X, the TV is something you just have on. For a generation raised on the simple plot lines and musical underpinnings of *The Brady Bunch, Happy Days,* and *Welcome Back Kotter,* MTV provides a type of soothing Muzak. For Boomers and Builders such an environment is discomfiting. Previously, older generations employed the radio for background music to their daily tasks. When Boomers and their parents watched television, they sat in front of the television and gave shows such as *The Dick Van Dyke Show, The Ed Sullivan Show,* or *Your Show of Shows* their undivided attention, much the same way as they sat in a theatre. But, MTV became the new and raw visual radio of Generation X. It carries more than a radio or televised variety show ever could, for it provides a rapid succession of edgy images of success, sex, and euphoria.

As a result, Generation X may be more cosmopolitan, more urbane, more sensual, and more tolerant than its forebears. A broad range of issues, from apartheid to sexual abuse, is addressed minute-by-minute in a shower of color, images, and icons, all the while accompanied by catchy melodies and enticing lyrics. Those regularly exposed to these images will prefer rapid and colorful presentations, quite the opposite of the manner in which most of our churches present the good news.

The Personality of Generation X: Global Citizens

Those in Generation X have been raised in a world of international trade, commerce, and tension. Thus, they understand that their duty is to be good global citizens. Generation X was nurtured on the charity megaconcerts of the 1980s, such as "Live Aid Concerts" to address the famine in Africa, or "Farm Aid Festivals" to aid the impoverished family farm in America. To Generation X, it was rock musicians, not Christians, who saw the need and quickly raised money to alleviate the suffering. Though the Christian church already had in place many programs to address these situations, the church was not as adept at harnessing the media. As a result, Generation X was given the impression that the church was caught napping.

Most Generation X musicians seem to have a favorite charity or popular cause, and Generation X perceives itself as a righter of wrong in the global community. Heroes like Nelson Mandela and Mother Teresa are eagerly embraced by the youth culture, while Christian relief organizations, such as Franklin Graham's organization, Samaritan's Purse, go largely unnoticed.

To make the world a better place is no longer perceived to be the sole responsibility of religious organizations. Global partnership and charity is now a secular responsibility, and the church's cultural mandate from Jesus to care for "one of these brothers of mine, even the least of them," is regrettably under appreciated.

Generation X: Their Views of Boomers

Generation X largely sees Baby Boomers across the same generation gap that distorts the Boomer view. Opinions formed while gazing across a generation gap are usually distorted and stereotypical. Generation X is not really the bust or the "X" that Boomers thought. The same distortions afflict the Gen-X view of Boomers.

Boomers are perceived by Generation X to be self-absorbed and success driven. The proliferation of broken homes, created by their parents' quest for success, has soured many Gen-Xers to the pursuit of prosperity. Those in the younger generation largely want a comfortable existence with a moderate level of living, in which they can also be comfortable with their social responsibility. They want to feel that they are making a positive contribution to solving the injustices of the world, and at the same time, giving needed attention to their spouses and offspring. It is little wonder that Generation X is putting off marriage and having children until later in life, rather than following the example of their amply reproductive parents.

Subsequently, Generation X views Boomer ideas and suggestions with a measure of suspicion. It will cautiously appraise Boomer ideas, and hold them up in comparison to its own ideas of fairness, justice, and integrity. Although the Boomers are their bosses, their pastors, and their teachers, the Gen-Xers are not content to let the Boomers call the shots. They suspect Boomer motives, perhaps with good reason, and as such, Gen-Xers must be allowed to participate in the decision-making process or they will not possess goal ownership.

Generation X: Their Views of Builders and Seniors

The news is more hopeful when analyzing the Generation X attitude toward Builders, that generation which built the United States into a worldwide military and economic power. Often the existence of two generation gaps between generations means that the generations will be closer in outlook to each other than the generation in the middle. In other words, Generation Xers will probably have more values in common with the Builder generation than they will with their immediate progenitors, the Boomers. This phenomenon arises because, while the Boomers rebelled against their parents, the Builders, Generation X is rebelling against the Boomers. The rebellion of Generation X can be a return to some of the values of their grandparents, the Builders.

For example, the Boomers often rejected mainline churches, feeling they were too liturgically restrictive and resistant to change. As a result, Boomers chose the flexibility and creativity of independent churches. However, while growing up in the independent churches of their parents, Generation X often witnessed church splits and closures due to lack of ecclesiastical oversight. Thus, it is not surprising that Generation Xers often find mainline denominations more acceptable than their parents did. Researcher George Barna discovered that Generation X has a substantially more positive than negative view of the Catholic Church, Protestant churches, Baptist churches, Jewish congregations, and United Methodist churches.[5]

This appreciation for mainline churches is most likely due to the stability denominational affiliation provides. The rapidity with which Generation Xers witnessed the dissolution of their parents' independent churches, has led Generation X to value denominational ties. While at one time it was considered good strategy to remove the denominational title from church signage, it may now be prudent to retain such designations, if Generation X is being recruited.

What Generation X Is Looking for in a Church

There, of course, is no such thing as a church that meets the needs of all Gen-Xers. However, there are some characteristics of size, affiliation, emphasis, worship styles, and worship frequency that are very attractive to this generation.

Size: 200 to 300 people. Members of Generation X prefer the intimacy they missed while attending their parents' megachurches. Even if their parents did not attend a large church, they probably attended one that was to a certain degree obsessed with becoming large. The "bigger is better" mentality of the Boomers has left Generation X with the opinion that cohesion is preferred.

Denominational Affiliation: Mainline. The rationale for the Gen-X preference for a mainline denomination has been addressed above.

Emphasis: Rather than primarily emphasizing the needs

of the congregation, the Gen-X church emphasizes the needs of the community. This is an outgrowth of the philosophy of global citizenry. The needs of the poor and disenfranchised surely outweigh the needs of the majority of our congregants. A church that can take its place as a font of integrity, equality, and charity will address the Gen-X desire for moral responsibility.

Worship Styles: Gen-Xers prefer a church that offers both contemporary and traditional music. Generation X persons find value in the great songwriting and hymnology of their grandparents. Perhaps due to the lack of classical music in their parents' contemporary services, they often demonstrate a new-found appreciation for the hymns.

Yet, although they relish traditional hymns, they enjoy contemporary music to an even greater degree. Thus, when it comes to music, Generation X may possess the quintessential Renaissance spirit: appreciating many artistic forms simultaneously. However, this does not mean that the answer is a service which "blends" both contemporary songs and traditional hymns in the same service. Researcher Charles Arn believes that such blended services are usually too disjointed to please most people.[6] It seems that Gen-Xers prefer a church that offers separate opportunities for both traditional and contemporary music. Then, Generation X does not have to forfeit opportunities for either taste in music.

Service Times: Flexible and Varied. Gen-Xers are busy. In today's inflated economy, they will probably have to work harder than their parents to attain the same standard of living. With the disappearance of job security and the globalization of the marketplace, they find it necessity to work two or more jobs to attain economic stability. Coupled with this is a deification of customer service, resulting in more businesses open around the clock and seven days a week. As a result there are no time periods acceptable to all potential churchgoers. As a result, churches that offer varied times for church services can reach out more effectively to Generation X.

The Baby Boomers: A Term That Won't Go Away

While Generation X initially appears to have rejected its name because it was given by its parents, Boomers have no one to blame but themselves for their designation. The term "Boomer," conferred by a Boomer-led media, though displeasing has stuck. No other rival has emerged. And to Boomers who like to think of themselves as sophisticated, refined, and genteel, the homespun designation "Boomer" is an enigma.

The Personality of Boomers: Hanging Up or Hanging On?

Gail Sheehy has become a pop-historian of the Baby Boomer generation. When the Boomers were first entering their forties, Sheehy penned her successful book *New Passages* in which she extolled the virtues of the "Flourishing Forties." Despite being supported by all of the marketing prowess of its publisher, the book did not sell as expected. Shortly thereafter, there appeared a book written by academic writer Delia Ephron. Titled *Hanging Up*, this book was a morality tale of the angst-driven Boomer. Unexpectedly, this latter book tapped into anguish of the Baby Boomer and was an overnight success.

Ephron's premise is that the Baby Boomer is being both helped and tormented by technology in the quest to bridge the generation gaps. The telephone serves as a metaphor for mechanization gone mad. The heroine in *Hanging Up* simultaneously juggles duties of moving up the corporate ladder, caring for an invalid father, and parenting a defiant child. All of these responsibilities seem to be conducted primarily over the phone. The telephone, which makes communication across long distances possible, does not help the heroine cope with generational chasms between herself, her father, and her son. The only answer for the Boomer, theorizes Ephron, is to "hang up," and give up; or "hang on" and plod ahead. As a result, a bewildered Baby Boomer usually reluctantly forges ahead with a sense of anguish and woe, timidly forging across the generational chasm whenever possible.

Amid this insecurity, the Boomer generation finds itself the first consumer-driven generation. While their parents fought to establish the West as the dominant economic and military force in the world, the Boomer became an expert on consuming, due to its prosperity. The Boomers, unlike their parents, never knew the scarcity of a Great Depression. The Boomer never experienced a successful war to liberate enslaved masses cringing beneath the hand of totalitarian regimes. The Boomer, lacking such character-building experiences, matured in an era of prosperity and abundance.

However, maturing in a time of peace and prosperity allowed the Boomer to discover new ways to improve upon everything. America became the world's bread basket, the chief exporter of democracy, a global policeman, and the fountainhead for worldwide missionary endeavors. The Boomer took the accomplishments of his or her parents and improved them. Boomers updated and modernized the foundation the Builders had established.

But, herein lies the dilemma that afflicts many Boomers. While they could improve upon almost all technological relationships, they found themselves at a loss to similarly improve upon intergenerational relationships. Divorce skyrocketed, teen suicide increased, and substance abuse proliferated. Although eventually the walls of the Iron Curtain were ground to dust, the walls separating the generations remained as pronounced as ever. Success in so many technological endeavors, followed by widespread failures in the area of interpersonal relationships, disheartened the Boomer. To use Delia Ephron's metaphor, technological marvels such as the telephone became a symbol of the Boomer's relational failures.

Boomers: Their Views of Generation X

The Boomers have a surprisingly higher regard for Generation X than the latter appear to have for them. Remember, the Boomers are the first consumer-driven generation. And, in a world where advertising equates youth with beauty, it is little wonder that Baby Boomers look to younger generations for fashion, style, and inspiration.

It is not uncommon to find middle-aged Boomers sporting moderated versions of the clothing styles marketed to youth. The haircuts, accessories, and brand names that shout "youth" are finding their way into the closets of Boomers. Bombarded daily with televised images extolling the fashionableness of young people, Boomers prefer to dress more like their children than their parents.

Because of this yearning for a sip from the fountain of youth, Boomers are more likely to be attracted to Generation X events than *vice versa*. Generation X is more apt to view Boomer participation as a degradation of its style, rather than flattery. The Boomer, nurtured on consumerism, usually perceives little of this hostility, viewing imitation as the sincerest form of flattery.

Therefore, churches that offer Generation X ministries designed by a Boomer leadership will usually offer what a true Generation Xer will regard as counterfeit. For ministry to Generation X to be successful, the Boomer must relinquish control and allow Gen-Xers to design their own ministries and strategies.

Boomers: Their Views of Builders

The generation gap is most pronounced between the Boomers and the Builders. As mentioned above, the Boomer's tutoring at the hands of consumerism has produced an individual far different from his or her parents. The Builders appreciated the virtue of hard work, and worked at something because the task was self-fulfilling. Boomers, on the other hand, saw their job as improving their lot in life. While the Builder would sacrifice all for a worthy goal, the Boomer would sacrifice only when an improvement could be identified and quickly attained.

While their parents held tightly to the traditions they had grown up with, Boomers believe that everything can be improved. Thus, Boomers are optimistic and positive—sometimes too much so. A Boomer can sometimes operate beyond his or her level of expertise, because of an underlying feeling that everything is possible and anything can be improved. As such, the Boomer is driven by experimentation.

The Boomer is willing to try new ideas, but wants a careful record to be kept to verify that improvements have been attained. The approach of their parents that one's word was sufficient for verification, now is relinquished to a hardnosed assessment of the facts. Little wonder that the Church Growth Movement and its emphasis upon diagnostic analysis has been embraced by the Boomer—and little wonder it often puzzles the Builder.

Boomers look for quality in the work performed. Again, because of their consumerist influences, they want high quality as the end result. To a Boomer, the desire or effort given to a task is no substitute for quality in the outcome. However, with the Builder, work was judged on whether it was self-fulfilling. In other words, for the Builder, the heart of the person should be considered and this should supersede any resultant quality. In a Builder church, for example, a mediocre singer might be encouraged and lauded because of the sincere effort he or she was putting into the endeavor. However, in a church seeking to attract Boomers, such indifference to quality could alienate the Boomer. The Boomer wonders why the end product is not on a quality level that brings glory to God. But the Builder sees the effort as that which brings glory. In actuality, which brings glory? They both do.

What Boomers Are Looking for in a Church

Size: Boomers often feel bigger is better and usually look for a church of 300+ in size. After all, isn't an organization that can pool its resources better poised to produce a quality product? This attitude is largely a result of the globalization and industrialization of the marketplace after World War II. Prior to 1940, many companies were small business, producing a specialized product that a larger corporation would purchase in order to construct a larger piece of machinery. World War II changed all of that. The threat of global domination by Axis powers that rapidly nationalized major industries, flung the Western world into chaos. In order to keep pace with the armament of the Axis powers, American companies consolidated and merged. In the new corporate environment, raw materials, individual parts, and quality control could produce an end product more quickly and efficiently. The small garage and storefront manufacturing shops were purchased, consolidated, and made a small cog in the new megacorporations of the 1950s. While Builders might miss the autonomy and quality that a small workshop might offer, the Boomer believed that bigger was better.

Soon this penchant for bigness invaded the church. And, in certain areas, bigger really is better. Staff became better trained, a large church could often have a greater impact on the social consciousness of a community, and church workers could be paid a livable wage. However, the loss of intimacy in a large church would undermine the support of Builders, who saw the church as increasingly success driven and impersonal. Boomers, on the other hand, attested to improvements in ministry quality and quantity.

Boomers became accustomed to the broad range of ministries a large church could offer. They looked for churches that offered varied ministries, quality sermonizing, modern facilities, and masterful music. Music in many ways has always been the standard-bearer for a church. As such, music in

Boomer churches is professional, contemporary, and energetic. This has led some Builders and Generation Xers to feel the Boomer church has been held captive by a cult of success. Whether captive to their successfulness, or driven by a desire to adapt and improve, Boomers created churches that were bigger and more professional than ever before.

Denominational affiliation: Boomers prefer nonaffiliated churches. Boomers prefer the flexibility and autonomy that a church without a denominational affiliation affords. However, as mentioned earlier, this can lead to schisms and church breakups if accountability is missing.

Emphasis: Boomer churches emphasize the needs of the congregants over, but not in lieu of, the needs of those outside the church. Boomer churches are not coldhearted toward the plight of the world's disenfranchised. Many Boomer congregations have viable local and global social action strategies. However, they do feel that the needs of the church members are important and sometimes overlooked. This is the result of their experience in their parents' churches, where the needs of ministry sometimes took precedence over the needs of those ministering. Subsequently, the Boomer looks for a church that can offer self-help groups, leadership training, and lessons one can readily apply to one's own life. They are not unduly selfish, only overly sensitive to their own personal need.

Worship style: Boomers prefer a contemporary worship style. Boomers are the first generation raised with easy access to an abundance of music. Their parents, on the other hand, had to sometimes travel for hours to ballrooms and dancehalls to hear musical entertainment. The Boomer had only to flick a switch on a transistor radio to hear the best and latest music of the day. The phenomenal diffusion across the airwaves of rock and roll music soon made this musical genre an anthem for a generation. The generation that proudly invented its own form of music was not going to retreat to its parents' musical styles, even in the church.

Service Times: Flexible and Varied. Here the Boomers are very similar to their offspring, Generation X. They too look for churches offering several options for worship times. Their busy schedules—family responsibilities along with two wage earners in the family—means there is no longer any one given time that will be convenient for a majority of Boomers.

Builders and Seniors: Why World War II Is Important to Them

There is one generation that is more misunderstood than all others. It is a generation that has been lionized, as well as being castigated, for being too concerned with brick and mortar. Which is this often maligned and frequently misunderstood generation—Generation X or the Boomers? Neither. It consists of those people born in or before 1945, and known as the Builder Generation.

The Builders are a generation born between 1927 and 1945, who "built" the United States into a superpower, both economically and militarily. The high-water mark for this generation occurred more than fifty years ago, when they returned to their ancestral homelands in balsa wood gliders, dark green parachutes, and on easily capsizable landing craft. It was D day, the beginning of an invasion of what Adolf Hitler had declared was an impregnable "Fortress Europe." On that day, American builders were determined to prove once and for all that they were superior to the legendary master-builders of Europe. Their enormous accomplishments and self-sacrifice, led news commentator Tom Brokow to call this group the "Greatest Generation" in his book by the same title. A preference for selflessness and hard work, burnished by the fires of war, had forged these men and women of varied nationalities into the most resolute and forceful generation the world has ever seen.

Why Houses of Worship Are Important to Them

Builders have taken pride in the accomplishments of their hard work. In many ways, this Builder attitude is a result of a Northern European work ethic. On the European continent, the grandest artistic accomplishment is the Christian cathedral. Cathedrals are the result of the best artisans coming together from across a region to offer their finest work on a combined product. A European cathedral stood as an example of the best craftsmanship of a region. The best stonemasons crafted the statuary and walls; the best architects designed the delicate flying buttresses that would support massive stone roofs—the best woodworkers crafted the intricate symbols on the altar pieces; and the best glass artisans painstakingly created enormous stained-glass windows. Because craftsmanship was so important, time was not. Some cathedrals, such as the imposing Cologne Cathedral, would take hundreds of years to complete, being worked upon by successive generations of craftsmen. These wondrous architectural marvels were the work of the best craftsmen of their day. And to most craftsmen, this was the way they showed their devotion and worship—by giving to God's house their best work.

The church edifice is important to Builders steeped in this heritage. Today, Builders gravitate toward volunteer positions in our churches that maintain the building. They see their involvement in the board of trustees, building committees, and maintenance committees as an outgrowth of their spirituality and devotion. To a Builder, keeping the house of God clean and in working order is a very laudable form of worship. They recognize their skills as God-given; thus, the craft of their hands becomes worship, when bestowed upon God's house.

This, of course, is a point that widens the chasm between Builders and Boomers. Boomers see the functionality and modernity of God's house as preeminent, since they have been tutored by consumerism. A Boomer wants a church that is accessible, flexible, and utilitarian. Boomer churches often crop up in warehouses, barns, movie theaters, and other such functional venues. The Builder congregation, on the other hand, prefers buildings with beautiful woodwork, stained glass, and magnificent masonry. The Boomer criticizes this fondness as worldly, materialistic, and carnal. In essence, however, nothing could be further from the truth. For many Builders, a beautiful and well-maintained house of God is a testimony of their devotion to God.

Are Seniors Builders?

The Senior Generation, those born prior to 1926, embrace many of the attitudes and preferences of their children, the Builders. This is not surprising, since Builders, when asked if they try to be like their parents, usually respond in the affirmative. When Boomers are asked the same question, they find the thought illogical, if not offensive.

Thus, a sizable generation gap does not appear to exist between the Senior and Builder generations, as it clearly does between the Boomer and Builder generations. Therefore, for the sake of clarity and simplicity, we shall continue considering the dwindling Senior Generation a segment of the much larger Builder generation. When referring to Builders we shall be including those persons born before 1926.

Builders: Their View of Boomers

Builders, like Generation X, view Boomers with a healthy dose of suspicion. Builders feel Boomers have lost touch with the soul of an organization. They feel Boomers see only the surface, and not the heart of an issue. When a Builder looks at a large aging edifice, they see the hundreds of person-hours that went toward making this building what it is today. Even in a decrepit state, Builders can see in their mind's eyes the workmen that repaired the roof, painters lovingly applying coats of paint, and masons setting the cornerstone. To a Builder, a structure never loses it character, for its essence is beneath the surface amid the many selfless deeds that went into making what this building was—and is.

The Boomer, on the other hand, sees a building past its prime and in need of removal to make way for the future. The Boomer wants a more user-friendly edifice, seeing only the aging structure's many impediments to increased ministry. The Boomer will readily remove a piece of altar furniture, or paint over some stained woodwork, never realizing that their action strikes at the core of worship for the Builder.

To sum up this difference, we might say that the Builder worships in part through the work of his or her hands. The Boomer, however, worships through a constant dedication to improvement and enhancement. Who is right? Which form of worship is the most valid?

Our experience in consulting hundreds of churches has led us to believe that both forms of worship are not only valid, but logical. Where would the Boomer be without the attention to craftsmanship of the Builder? Where would the Builder be without the Boomer's relentless pursuit of improvement?

The conflict arises when one perspective tries to dominate the other. Consequently, what we are advocating in the Tri-Gen format is a healthy respect for generational differences. We believe that only when all generations respect the differences inherent in different age groups can we foster a climate that will grow a Tri-Gen church.

Builders: Their View of Generation X

Builders are remarkably fond of Generation X. They find they have much in common with their grandchildren, including an appreciation for denominational ties. Builders also find that Generation X appreciates the oral history that the Builders possess. Unlike the era of the Boomers, which they experienced firsthand, Generation X savors the historical portal that their grandparents give to a bygone era. Margaret Mead suggests that "it [culture] depends for continuity upon the expectations of the old, and upon the almost ineradicable imprint of those expectations upon the young."[7]

In addition, it seems that passing across two generation gaps (the gap between Gen X and the Boomers, and the gap between the Boomers and Builders) often reverses the effect of the gaps. In other words, the things that one generation rebels against may be embraced by their children. Thus a generation twice removed, like Generation X, may actually hold options more similar to their grandparents than their parents.

Builders may be able to provide a natural link to Generation X. Builders seem more intuitive when relating to Generation X, and often are less swayed by Gen-X stereotypes. Therefore, churches seeking to reach Generation X, may be more successful utilizing Builders to staff these ministries than by using ostracized Boomers.

What Builders Are Looking for in a Church

Size: Builders prefer a church of under 300 in weekly attendance. Builders are very similar to Generation X in preference for church size. They see the church as operating most efficiently when it is not too small (seventy-five or less) and not too big (three hundred or more). Many Builders will fondly recount the glory days of their congregation, usually sometime in the first half of the twentieth century when many of their churches flourished in the two hundred to three hundred range.

Denominational affiliation: Builders prefer a church with a denominational affiliation. Aging Builders are encountering more uncertainty in their lives. They increasingly worry about the adequacy of their income and their ability to live on their own. Couple this with a dwindling circle of friendships, and you can see that aging Builders are looking for the stability that the Body of Christ can provide. Denominational traditions, liturgy, and programs lend a sense of security during an increasingly insecure time.

Emphasis: Builders want a church that emphasizes the importance of their heritage and opinions. Builders are greatly afraid of losing their churches to Boomers. Many of those interviewed have told stories of churches where aging members were slowly but steadily pushed aside in favor of progress. Builders, who have given so much to their church over a protracted period of time, are worried that soon they will not recognize their church. In the name of progress, they are afraid of losing one of the things most dear to them in their old age—their church.

Thus, Builders are looking for a church where they can give input. One thing that drives younger generations away is when they feel their input is not heeded. The same is true for the Builder. In the name of modernization, they fear their advice and experience will be ignored. They worry that decisions will be made for them without their input, and their church life will eventually resemble a prison where all of their decisions are made for them. Therefore, Builders want to have input, at least over their own affairs. They may initially struggle with relinquishing control to younger generations, but eventually will allow young people some control. But, Builders will continue to fight unyieldingly to control their own destiny. Builders want a church where they can, at the very least, control their own generation-specific forms of worship and ministry.

Worship styles: Builders prefer the worship styles they have become accustomed to. Builders are looking for churches where they are allowed to sing the hymns, practice the liturgy, and teach the Sunday school curriculum that, through familiarity, have added stability to their lives.

Worship times: Builders prefer Sunday morning. In the

twilight of their years, where death, infirmity, and separation of loved ones proliferate, Builders seek a church that offers an anchor of stability and familiarity amidst the cultural storms. Therefore, Builders prefer churches where worship is conducted in their church's traditional manner, and at the traditional time. They fear that even small inroads of contemporary elements will one day become a flood that washes away all the traditions dear to them.

When considering figure 3.1 remember, the "ideal" church does not exist. This comparison is only a way to demonstrate a difference in general preferences. Among every age group there are many exceptions. After a brief discussion of Generation Y, we will look at some generational exceptions that can either help or hinder, depending on how they are utilized.

Figure 3.1 What Generations Are Looking for in a Church: A Comparison

	Generation X	Boomer	Builders
Size	200–300	300+	75–300
Affiliation	mainline denomination	independent	mainline denomination
Emphasis	needs of the community	needs of the congregation	need to be heard
Worship Style	traditional & contemporary	contemporary	traditional
Worship Times	flexible & varied	flexible & varied	Sunday morning

No Gen-Y?

Occasionally, in this book, we have alluded to the most recent generation born, and called it "Generation Y." Keeping within the nineteen-year generational spans favored by sociologists, this generation can be thought of as those born in and between 1984 and 2002. As of yet, there is no designation for this generation that has attained widespread acceptance. Sometimes they are called "the millennials," since their birth years span the artificial demarcation line between two millennia. At other times, they are referred to as "the mosaics," because of the great variety of the influences that have come to bear upon them. Some social wags use the term "connectivity kids," since they are the first generation born into a society in which instant worldwide connectivity is common. However, the impertinence of this latter designation, coupled with its pubescent label, will probably mean that this generation will eschew this name in favor of another. However, as the Boomers learned, simply shunning a designation does not mean it will go away.

The label the authors prefer is one associated with the Generation X designation. Because this generation follows Generation X in birth order, and X is followed by Y in the alphabet, they are frequently called Generation Y. Although the final designation for this generation has not yet been decided, the simpler and less derisive "Generation Y" will be preferred in this book.

But what about their needs? Why are they not addressed fully in this present discussion? The authors have taken a long and circumspect look at this question. In the end, we have made an intentional decision not to include this generation in the present discussion, due to the social development and emotional metamorphosis that young people at this age undergo. They are a generation comprised primarily of adolescents and young adults. Subsequently, it will be a while longer before their predilections and penchants are systematized and codified, much less fully understood to the degree required in this present discussion. Their ideals and aspirations are still being molded by the pressures of childhood, puberty, adolescence, and young adulthood. To attempt to analyze them at this early stage, within the comparative parameters required in this book, would be premature. However, the authors look forward to exploring the ideals and aspirations of this, and subsequent generations, in future books on the subject.

Exceptions to the Rules: Cross-Generational Surfers

Builders Who Don't Build

Throughout the evening, a small dissenting voice arose from the back of the room. The parlor had been filled with concerned members of this dwindling congregation. Each attendee brought his or her own analysis of why this once thriving church of more than three hundred now managed to muster fewer than forty in worship. Many thought that younger generations lacked the spiritual sensitivity of their parents, while others claimed that the intemperance of youth was the root of their absence.

Amid these denunciations, a thin voice regularly emerged from the last row, each time defending the younger generation as sincere, spiritual, and simply misunderstood. I noticed the voice came from a kindly gray-haired man who looked very much like the other senior citizens. But, this gentleman's perspective was definitely not that of his peers. He held an outlook on the younger generation of respect, sympathy, and even admiration. Though a number of persons agreed with him, most of the louder voices scoffed— but, he held his ground. At the close of the evening, I made my way to the back of the parlor to meet this elderly man. As I approached, he turned to leave, and I noticed something of which I had been unaware. I noticed his silver hair was neatly pulled into a mid-shoulder length ponytail.

This man became one of the leading voices in a church that would soon reach out to the young people moving into this semi-urban area. He always seemed to have the best interests of the younger generation in mind. And, he seemed intuitively to understand their needs and their customs. Soon, he had marshaled similar like-minded Builders around him. As I came to know this gray-haired retiree, I discovered he had more in common with Generation X than with his own generation.

Over the years, I have witnessed this same phenomenon many times. However, often they don't have such noticeable fashion features. But, they do share one thing in common, and that is an unswerving allegiance, understanding, and love for another generation. The result is often that they feel more at home in another generation, than in their own. Such individuals become important voices in a church that is seeking to understand the younger generations. This gentleman's ideas, input, and advice became a key factor in this church's journey back to health. His relationship with his peers, forged over time, provided an important bedrock and validation for his suggestions and ideas.

New understandings of church structure, such as in the Tri-Gen model, require new terminology. Thus, people who more readily relate to another generation than their own the authors have dubbed, "cross-generational surfers." The imagery of surfing carries the fluid nature of their crossover. In addition, it is a reminder that though they appear at home, they are not in their natural environment, any more than a land dweller is naturally at home upon the surf. Thus, the cross-generational surfer is a key player in a congregation that seeks to understand and assimilate a younger culture. The cross-generational surfer who operates from a sincere affection for another generation can be a wellspring of ideas and a sounding board of appropriateness.

Boomers Who Think They Are Gen-Xers

The cross-generational surfer is not limited to the Builder, for its most frequent manifestation is found in the Boomer. As mentioned earlier, the Boomer looks youthward, rather than to forefathers, for inspiration. Subsequently, it is not

uncommon for Boomers to so identify with the youth culture that they surf cross-generationally into its midst. Such
generational surfers often adopt the fashion, jargon, and
even occupations of the youthful culture. In a commercial
world where success is linked with youth, such surfers are
often media darlings. Hollywood and the music industry
continually paint a picture of the ideal Boomers looking and
acting like their youthful counterparts.

Many of these individuals sincerely identify with another
generation, and like the Builder surfers, they can become
sources for advice, ideas, and guidance. A church that possesses such individuals will find them invaluable in reaching
younger generations.

However, one word of caution is in order. Ever since psy-
chologist Erik Erikson discovered that people pass through
certain "phases" as they age, one phase has been particularly
troublesome. This is the phase identified as the "midlife crisis." Psychologists believe that a sudden mid-age onset of
cross-generational surfing can be caused by feelings of inadequacy and ineptitude. The rapid appearance of cross-
generational surfing at mid-age may be a signal that the individual feels he or she has failed in attaining one's life goals.
Thus, midlife surfing can be an attempt to recapture one's
youth and begin anew. Such reasons for cross-generational
surfing should disqualify someone from being an advisor.
Only generational surfers who do so naturally, sincerely, and
consistently should be sought out as cross-generational
ambassadors.

Generation Xers Who Defy Categorization

Among the vast Generation X demographic are many sub-
groups. However, one of the most important for the church
appears to be the new traditionalists. These are young people who hold to many of the beliefs of their grandparents.
They can be conservative in politics, morals, and outlook,

while still gravitating in fashion and style to their own generation. These new traditionalists are not always religious, but they are spiritual. They are attracted to spirituality in many forms—Eastern, mystic, Judeo-Christian, and intergalactic. Thus, their curiosity with Christianity should not be taken to indicate that they are ready to accept, or are even aware of, its tenets.

The new traditionalists are not really cross-generational surfers in the truest sense of the word. While they are attracted to the charity and temperance of Christianity, they may have little understanding of its core beliefs.[8] Thus, a new traditionalist should not immediately be given a central position of advice. The person may first need a measure of tutoring and mentoring.

However, if the person's curiosity is addressed, then the neotraditional Gen-Xer will more quickly join our churches than his or her peers. Thus, the new traditionalist can provide a foundation of understanding that can aid ministry to Generation X.

Utilizing cross-generational surfers is not without risk. But for the church that circumspectly uses such individuals, a beachhead may be quickly established in a generation that until now was beyond a congregation's reach.

Chapter Four

When $1 + 1 + 1 = 1$

The Strength of the Tri-Gen Church

He sat across the desk looking like a youthful Saint Nick. His round face, half hidden by a bushy, black beard, and his ample frame radiated both charm and impish playfulness. I could see why residents of this community were drawn to this pastor. But, as I interviewed him, I realized there was a deeper, more fundamental reason for the growth of the church he pastored. This pastor had embraced a Tri-Gen strategy and even fabricated a new equation to describe it.

"In our church, I tell them God's law of mathematics works differently from ours. In our world, $2 + 2 = 4$. But in God's math, $1 + 1 + 1 = 1$." This equation was this pastor's way of imparting the Tri-Gen strategy. "You see," he continued, "the Trinity follows the same mathematical law, $1 + 1 + 1 = 1$. And so, the church should not be surprised when the same formula applies to our generations. We may be three generations, but we are one body."

His church was growing with the Tri-Gen approach, and the mathematical formula appeared to help the congregants grasp the concept.

Defining the Tri-generational Model

In chapters 1 and 2, we briefly defined the tri-generational model. First, let us restate the definition:

> **Defining the Tri-Gen Church:**
> The tri-generational church is a holistic congregation with three distinct generational sub-congregations peacefully coexisting under one roof, one name, and one leadership core.

Now, let us look at this definition in more detail.

> **Defining the Tri-Gen Church:**
> The tri-generational church is *a holistic congregation* with three distinct generational sub-congregations peacefully coexisting under one roof, one name, and one leadership core.

A holistic congregation means that a tri-generational approach is a unified philosophy. It pervades every area of a church's ministry and structure. As noted in chapter 2, it is helpful to think of a balanced church structure as comprised of four areas of ministry. These areas can be thought of as four "Cs," and include:

- **Cultivate** spiritual growth through teaching ministries, often called Christian Education.
- **Care** for God's people through care giving, sometimes called Care or Compassion Ministries.
- **Communicate** Christ's love through outreach ministry; often these are Evangelism or Mission Departments.
- **Celebrate** God's goodness through worship, or what is better known as Worship Ministries.

For the tri-generational strategy to aid an aging church, every area of a church must embrace a tri-generational philosophy. The envisioning process, outlined in the following chapter, allows each department of a church to draft a ministry plan that embraces a Tri-Gen outlook.

Defining the Tri-Gen Church:
The tri-generational church is a holistic congregation *with three distinct generational sub- congregations* **peacefully coexisting under one roof, one name, and one leadership core.**

With three distinct generational sub-congregations means that a Tri-Gen church is comprised of three generations, each with distinctly different ideals and aspirations. It might be helpful to further define ideals and aspirations.

- Distinct *ideals* means that a generation possesses its own unique idea of *ideal* beauty and conduct. For the Gen-Xer, beauty could be spiked hair, multiple necklaces, and baggy jeans. For a Builder ideal beauty would be something quite different. For the Boomer, an ideal action might be to work hard and get ahead. Yet, for the Gen-Xer, ideal action might be a proper balance between vocation and family responsibility. Ideals carry the concept of what a person labels the epitome of beauty and conduct.
- Embracing different *aspirations* means we possess different goals to which we aspire. A member of Generation X might aspire to forge an identity separate from that of one's parents. A Boomer might aspire to lay the foundation for a new start-up enterprise. A Builder also might aspire to retire and live comfortably on one's life savings. These three examples are based upon a pursuit of the same thing, *security*, but each manifests itself through different aspirations.

If a pastor were delivering a sermon to these three groups simultaneously, the sermon might have to have three separate applications to meet the different needs, or aspirations, of each generation. Thus, it becomes clear that, in each generation, the search for different ideals and aspirations leads to different routes toward happiness. Conflict arises when one generation projects its ideals and aspirations upon another generation. This is usually done in a well-meaning effort to help, but the result is that the generation gap widens, and eventually, an extensive rift develops between generations.

Defining the Tri-Gen Church:
The tri-generational church is a holistic congregation with three distinct generational sub-congregations *peacefully coexisting* **under one roof, one name, and one leadership core.**

Peacefully coexisting is, therefore, essential for the success of the Tri-Gen church.

- Peaceful coexistence *begins* with a hearty respect for the different ideals and aspirations of each generation. Teachings, case studies, one-on-one nurturing, or a visitation of the Holy Spirit may be necessary to impart this respect.
- Peaceful coexistence *matures* by developing tolerance for new ideas, fashion, and ways of doing things. Being able to demonstrate the appropriateness and soundness of new ideas is not only helpful, but also necessary.
- Moreover, peaceful coexistence *culminates* by employing bridge-building exercises that will relieve the inevitable generational friction. E. Steve Eidson in *When Lines Are Drawn: A Guide to Resolving Conflict in the Church* suggests the best type of conflict management in the church is the collaborative approach. In

this approach, goals of both parties are preserved, often with parallel solutions (collaboration) rather than the typical approach in which each side gives up something meaningful (compromise). Eidson warns that "even though this style of conflict management (compromise) has been touted as the most effective means of dealing with problems, there are shortcomings.... [When] goals are always developed around the bargaining table, the end result is value confusion and a climate of suspicion."[1]

Only in a collaborative approach to conflict management, where both parties' opinions are respected and not mutually exclusive, can harmony, trust, and openness emerge. Collaborative conflict management thus adds new programming ideas, rather than eliminating traditions or creating a hybrid.

> **Defining the Tri-Gen Church:**
> The tri-generational church is a holistic congregation with three distinct generational sub-congregations peacefully coexisting *under one roof,* one name, and one leadership core.

Under one roof means that most Tri-Gen churches, and especially those under two hundred in Sunday attendance, will most easily grow if they coexist in the same church facility. This is because a Tri-Gen approach makes better use of the existing church facility. The necessity for parallel ministries in the tri-generational church means that smaller activities will be going on at more times. Using the same building at different hours becomes wise stewardship of the church's facilities.

This approach often is seen when churches of different ethnicities rent the same church building. It is not uncommon in metropolitan areas to find an aging congregation renting out their building to a different ethnic church on early Sunday morning and then to another ethnic congregation on Sunday evening. The practical implications for the multiple use of the sanctuary and Sunday school rooms helps all three groups. The tri-generation approach does the same thing, only with generational sub-congregations rather than with separate ethnically defined churches. Multiple use by different generations allows each group to contribute its finances and person-power to the improvement and upkeep of the facility.

However, "under one roof" in our definition can also be used in a figurative sense. Some congregations, due to growth, find it necessary to develop separate buildings or campuses to minister to a burgeoning congregation. In this circumstance, the Builder sub-congregation might wish to continue to hold services in a traditional edifice, while the younger generations erect a multipurpose facility. These buildings may be on the same campus, or due to lack of land, may be at a different site. In either circumstance, the mental picture of "under one roof" must be preserved in order to retain unity and cohesiveness. When a congregation pictures itself as under one roof, even symbolically, a tendency toward separateness, sectarianism, and partisanship is less likely.

> **Defining the Tri-Gen Church:**
> The tri-generational church is a holistic congregation with three distinct generational sub-congregations peacefully coexisting *under* one roof, *one name,* and one leadership core.

To assist in the mental picture of unity in the midst of multigenerational sub-congregations, the use of *one name* is helpful. A name often draws a connection with the history of a church. A name can signify what a church can be. Some churches have discovered it is not too hard to modify a name so that it embraces its history (a preference of Builders) while updating it to a degree for the Boomer and Gen-Xer. Figure 4.1 includes some examples:

Figure 4.1

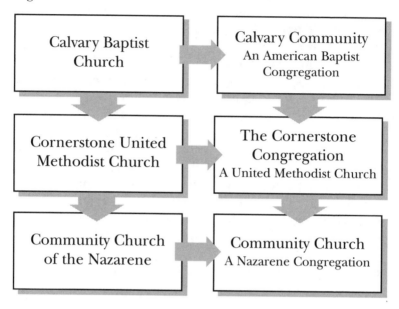

These modified names carried an air of informality, attractive to the younger generations, while still preserving a link to the historic past of the congregation.

Regardless of whether a church decides to update its name, a single name can be the communal glue that helps hold together the multigenerational congregation. However, be cautious when considering names that are identified solely with one emerging sub-congregation. In one church, the Boomer Bible Study known as the "Lighthouse" class grew until it was almost 20 percent of the Sunday morning attendance. During a vision-casting session with the church leadership, one young person remarked, "A lot of people in (town name) know the Lighthouse study. We could grow faster if we adopted the name Lighthouse Baptist Church rather than First Baptist." The speaker was unaware of the growing stares of consternation that crept across the faces of the Builders in the back of the room. Soon, a spate of hands flung into the air, offering to voice their displeasure at such an impertinent suggestion. The Builders could remember many years of fruitful ministry, and did not want to sacrifice that history upon the altar of progress.

After a protracted debate, and implementation of the "collaborative" style of conflict management, the church agreed to designate a focus group of all three generations to come up with a suitable solution. Eight months later, the church unveiled a new sign. In bold letters was the church name "First Baptist Church," but immediately below this designation in letters almost as large was the byline, "A Lighthouse to the Tri-State Area." The focus group had collaborated on a name that gave honor to both the historical relevance of the church and the youthful influx it now enjoyed.

Defining the Tri-Gen Church:
The tri-generational church is a holistic congregation with three distinct generational sub-congregations peacefully coexisting *under* one roof, one name, and *one leadership core*.

Under one leadership core means that a Tri-Gen church will utilize a senior leadership "core," comprised of either a leadership team, committee/board, or pastor, depending on the church's tradition and polity. Often, in most of these approaches, one senior leader will emerge in the role of figurehead.

Regardless of composition, the senior leadership core must make the prayerful, yet final decision in the direction of the church, as the hand-lettered sign on Harry S Truman's desk once read, "The buck stops here." Even in the historically democratic structure of American

Protestantism, there must be a final authority. And this authority must meet the qualifications of leadership as outlined in 1 Timothy 3:1-13 and Titus 1:5-9, in addition to passing muster before the people he or she shepherds.

Sometimes, in the Tri-Gen church, two or more senior leaders will emerge with approximately the same responsibilities, only for different generations. A Generation X pastor may have shepherding, preaching, and administrative duties to the Gen-X sub-congregation. A Boomer pastor may have similar responsibilities to a Boomer sub-congregation. In this scenario, it is easy to see how rivalries and antagonism could develop. Thus, even in such circumstances, it is important to have a clearly defined authority structure.

Some Tri-Gen churches have tried copastors with limited success. Others have tried alternating senior leaders. In both scenarios, a lack of direction and focus have resulted. The church appears to need a senior leader at the top, in much the same way as a corporation needs a senior executive who can be depended on to call the shots. One qualified and commissioned senior leader seems to be prudent, even in the multifaceted environment of the Tri-Gen church.

What the Tri-generational Church Looks Like

In order for a church to become a tri-generational church, it must not only develop into three age sub-groupings, but must also include a complete leadership/ministry structure for each. To achieve a complete leadership/ministry structure, each generation must eventually have four components.

(1) Each generation must eventually have a *shepherd*, with whom they can publicly identify during events, worship, and ministry activities.

(2)   Each generation must eventually have a *lay shep-herding team,* comprised of members of their own age group. This leadership team, board, or committee is given general oversight for a specific generation. They must be trained with the skills to counsel and nurture within the context of their generation. They will also deploy and oversee ministries of interest to their age group. They will be accountable to both the shepherd of their age group, and to the senior leadership core.

(3)   Each generation must eventually have *its own ministries.* Ministry must develop aimed directly at generational interests and talents. These ministries must be sufficiently promoted so that all age sub-groupings can identify ministries, activities, and events relevant to their age group. However, these ministries must never be generationally exclusive, or they will discourage the cross-generational surfers who also need them.

(4)   Each generation must eventually have *its own artistic expression.* Personal artistic expression is a key ingredient of worship, and it is an important component of every generational sub-congregation. Usually, this artistic expression manifests itself through the musical idiom. People like to worship in an environment that is both familiar and engaging. Using musical forms that are familiar and well known creates contentment, security, and repose. We will consider the crucial role of worship more fully in chapter 8.

With the above leadership/ministry structure established, what then does the tri-generational church look like graphically? In figure 4.2, we will start by graphing how an individual generational sub-congregation might be organized.

This, then, is the leadership/ministry structure that might be found in each generational sub-congregation of

Figure 4.2

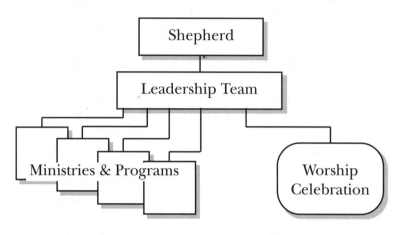

the Tri-Gen church. Figure 4.2 could describe a Generation X, Boomer, or Builder sub-congregation.

Remember, this is only what the leadership/ministry structure looks like for one generation. Let us now look at figure 4.3, which expands the above diagram for the three generations in a Tri-Gen church.

Figure 4.3 shows how the lines of accountability might flow in a church with a democratic form of government. In this example, the lay leadership team is directly linked to the leadership core. However, in some churches, it may be the shepherd who is the direct link between the leadership core and the lay leadership team. Regardless of the leadership style embraced, it is the parallelism of the tri-generational approach that is important to understand.

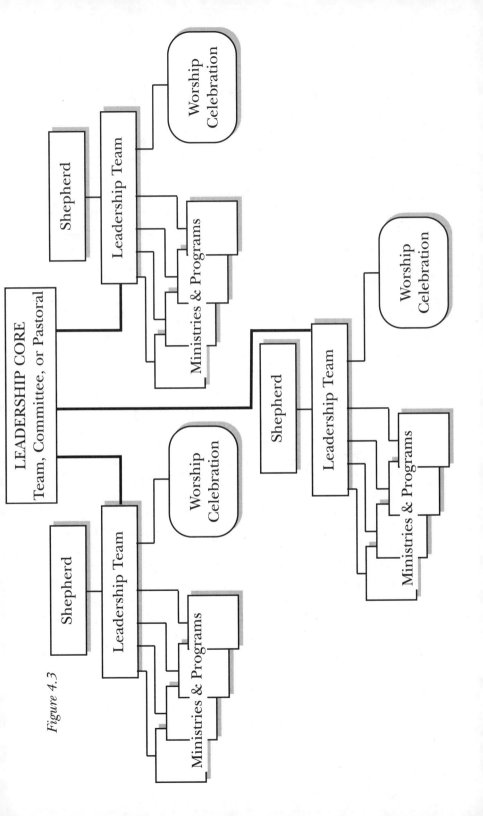

Figure 4.3

LEADERSHIP CORE
Team, Committee, or Pastoral

Shepherd

Leadership Team

Worship Celebration

Ministries & Programs

How the Tri-generational Church Produces Results

Physical Health

"In hindsight, they should have done things differently," confided the Boomer-aged pastor. "Ten years ago, our district planted a church three miles from here to reach out to singles, divorced people, and young parents. And, you have to pass by another church of our denomination to get there. Eventually, the new church became a church of Baby Boomers. Unfortunately, some of them were the young ones we needed to keep us going. Looking back, it sure doesn't seem like a very smart use of finances, staff, or people." This is an example of how the church planting strategy of the 1980s often went awry when generational differences in the local church were not addressed first. Often, denominational leaders saw the need to reach out to younger generations in a community. Rather than try to convert an aging congregation to a Tri- Gen format, it appeared easier to start a Boomer-oriented congregation nearby.

The shortsighted side of this approach often surfaced a few years later, when each church was struggling to grow. "It's not easy being a church plant with three other churches of our denomination nearby," observed the pastor of the planted offspring. "When we started, we didn't get the church support we needed, because we were viewed as competition rather than a complement. And when financially stable people of our denomination move to the city, they are not going to look here first. We have great people, but many are going through major life transitions such as divorce or career shifts. We have very little stability." Things were similarly frustrating at First Church. "We're rethinking how we should reach out to young people," shared the pastor of First Church. "It's the main focus of our work now."

The effects of being a predominantly one-generation church had affected both of these congregations. Today, First Church has regained some of the Boomers it lost. The .

planted church, on the other hand, which was launched with so much promise and fanfare, is clinging to survival, in a rented building with only a Boomer composition.

Planting churches to reach generations missing from the mother church will usually result in two churches in close proximity, each trying to support a staff, a building, and a ministry. Yet, if both of these churches were still part of the same entity, they would have enough combined resources to do the job right. "It may have been smart if First Church had just hired someone to reach out to Baby Boomers instead of this whole plant thing," the planted church pastor reflected. "I think a lot of our members would have rather done it that way." Hindsight always appears to be twenty-twenty.

The tri-generational strategy gives the aging congregation a youthful influx, and this youthful influx will enjoy the stability and strength of their progenitors. From utilization of facilities, to utilization of staff, the tri-generational approach offers a conservation and stewardship of resources.

Financial Health

The power years of vocational income are traditionally the mid forties to mid fifties. These are the years of economic prowess during which the average American wage earner can expect to earn the highest wage of his or her lifetime. In most areas of America, except for certain artificially inflated areas such as the Silicon Valley, this still holds true. Up until approximately ten years before an American worker retires, he or she can expect to be at the peak of his or her earnings.

After the mid fifties, however, earnings usually plateau. At retirement, income usually becomes fixed, and senior citizens must learn to stretch their resources to cover the rising cost of living. Below the mid forties, income may be increasing, but growing children and continuing education take an ever-increasing bite out of earnings.

Thus, the power years, that period between the mid forties and mid fifties where earnings are the highest and the expenses of raising children are waning, is one of the most important periods for funding ministry. Congregants in this age range provide a substantial, part of a church's budget on behalf of those who are earning less. But, let us offer a word of caution. We are not advocating that anyone be granted greater esteem or position because of the size of their giving. What we are observing is that the tithe (10 percent) of a member's income in the power years of earning may help fund ministry toward generations that are less prosperous at present.

This intergenerational dependence may be what God intended. In *Your Spiritual Gifts Can Help Your Church Grow,* Peter Wagner uses Romans 13:8 and 2 Corinthians 8:2 to expound upon the gift of giving. Wagner states "The gift of giving is the special ability that God gives to certain members of the body of Christ to contribute their material resources to the work of the Lord with liberality and cheerfulness."[2] Now, while this gift is by no means limited to those of resource, it certainly follows that God allows us to prosper, in part, so that we can fund the advance of His kingdom. The gifts of the Spirit, along with the presence of multigenerational congregants, may be what is necessary for the "whole body, joined and held together by every supporting ligament, grows and builds itself up in love, as each part does its work" (Ephesians 4:16).

Relational Health

"It was one of the best activities we ever planned," responded this Gen-Xer. As he spoke, he beamed with such enthusiasm that I almost forgot about his four earrings, which I had been uncomfortably staring at earlier. "Our church decided to have home groups on Sunday nights, and the young people and the old(er) people were the only ones that didn't want to participate." As his youthful wife stood nodding in agreement he continued, "We decided to have a combined event with the older people, and they were great. We have a lot in common, and it was the best event I can remember." "What did you discover that you had in common?" I asked. His countenance turned serious as he said, "Many of them got saved when they were my age. We talked a lot about how it's hard to be a Christian when your friends aren't. They really knew what it was like. I mean, I really got a lot of good advice from them. They rock!"

As we saw in the illustrations of chapter 2, the church that is primarily comprised of one generation often suffers from relational malfunction. The needed interaction between child, parent, and grandparent, which is so important for relational health, is missing. Without a multigenerational environment, our churches become enclaves of biases. Restricted in our outlook, and quick to stereotype those who are different, we can become bastions of dogmatism, ill will, and, at worst, prejudice.

Spiritual Health

There is an inherent spiritual healthiness that exudes from a church where three generations interact. Mature members of the church possess the insights that come from overcoming many trials and difficulties. These lessons of life, learned upon the pitching seas of calamity, can best be imparted to subsequent generations when three generations are present.

Margaret Mead stated that "It is true that the continuity of all cultures depends on the living presence of at least three generations."[3] By this, she meant that the beliefs, ethical code, and history of a culture are only passed down when there are three generations present. In this environment, the generation gap is successfully crossed when grandparents pass their stories, morals, and beliefs to their grandchildren.

This is because, as noted in the previous chapter, when beliefs pass across two generation gaps, such as between the Builders down to Generation X, the message stays relatively intact. This phenomena occurs because generations twice removed from one another are likely to have better communication lines than generations immediately adjacent. In other words, one generation rebels against their parents, and then their children rebel against them. Often the defiance of the grandchildren will bring them back to "ideals and aspirations" closer to that of their grandparents. Thus, while a parent may say something the child does not heed, the grandparent will more likely be able to say the same thing with greater reception.

Subsequently, the grandparent's generation may be the best mentor and tutor for the grandchild. A tri-generational church environment allows this mentoring relationship to develop fully. And, the admonitions of Paul to Titus to utilize the mature women in instructing the young women (Titus 2:3-5) certainly presupposes this multienerational approach.

Longevity

Without a doubt, the one-generation church is doomed without youthful influx. In chapter 1, we saw how many churches in America are dying. In chapter 2, we discovered the leading cause of this trend is "geriatrophy," the slow death of a church due to congregational old age.

The tri-generational approach, if continually embraced as new generations emerge, will mean that a church will always have the three generations needed for the transfer of morals and beliefs. Tri-Gen churches preserve their hallowed legacy and bridge successive generation gaps. If congregations are founded upon genuine respect and tolerance for the ideals and aspirations of each generation, they will be steadily resistant to generational strife and friction.

Why Didn't My Parents' Church Have This Problem?

This question usually arises when discussing generation gaps. However, a careful look at churches in the first half of the twentieth century will reveal that generation gaps were not as pronounced, and these gaps were crossed because families lived near each other.

When Generation Gaps Were Narrower

People in the early years of the twentieth century were not as exposed to niche marketing as they are today. Advertising was expensive. Billboards, newspaper ads, and signage were the primary methods of selling a product. Because of the cost and scarcity of these venues, niche marketing was not possible. Niche marketing is advertising aimed at a certain "niche," which might be an age-group, interest, or social strata. Prior to niche marketing, most advertising was general in appeal. A product might be targeted at farmers, factory workers, or office workers; but it would rarely be targeted at an age group or social strata.

Generations born in the first half of the twentieth century rebelled against their parents, and might sneak a cigarette, or squirrel away a bottle of alcohol. But, they would wear the same shoes, buy the same cigarettes, and drink the same liquor as their parents. Their rebellion led them to use things of their parents in a new way, but they did not adopt wholesale a different product. Their rebellion took the form of an adaptation of the resources of their parents' culture.

However, with the proliferation of the radio, then television, and finally the Internet, most advertising became niche marketing. The eighteen-to-twenty-four-year-old demographic sweet spot was unheard of prior to the 1960s. Today, this demographic is the golden goose of marketing legend.

When new marketing strategies appeared, designed to make each generation crave different ideals and aspirations, generations tended to pull apart. Musicians, the poetic troubadours of a generation, gave verse to these differences.

The result was that soon there emerged, and marketers could identify, very real differences in the ideals and aspirations of each generation. The generation gaps became more pronounced and more potent.

Families Living in Proximity

When families live in proximity, different generations learn to get along, due to familiarity and intimacy. Nearness is the great bridge-builder across the generational chasm. But, in the later half of the twentieth century, the extended family pulled apart.

While it was not unusual to have three generations of an extended family living under the same roof in 1900, this is the exception to the rule in most of North America in the new millennium. There are, of course, many people who must live in proximity, because of economic circumstances. Despite their hardship, they may be experiencing something many middle-class members of America are losing—a sense of family.

The nuclear family for many Americans is now blended and/or long distance. Many children are living far away, or are estranged from one of their biological parents. Grandparents now most often reside in retirement communities or sun-belt states. At one time, it was considered unseemly to relegate a parent to an institution for care, but now, it is almost the norm.

A complete review of all of the societal factors that have led to this dispersion of nuclear and extended families is beyond the scope of this book. However, it is important to recognize that the generation gaps have increased in potency, due to a lack of extended families living together in the same household or even in the same town, city, or state. Sadly, the prognosis is for the dispersion of the family to continue. As a result, the church has a contribution to make as a tri-generational refuge.

The Tri-Gen Model Is Necessary for the Survival of Smaller Churches

Special Needs of Churches with Fewer Than 200 Members

Awkward Size—Churches hovering around and a little under two hundred in attendance are labeled by Lyle Schaller as "awkward sized" congregations.[4] Though the authors generally prefer the more simple designations of small, medium, and large, Schaller's use of the term "awkward" is helpful to consider.

The awkward church is so labeled because to the pastor it feels awkward, although to the congregation it may be very comfortable. The pastor finds this church awkward because of the amount of work required. This size congregation is usually too small to afford a second pastor, but too large to be pastored by one shepherd. While this is seriously clear to the pastor trying to juggle a full schedule, the congregants often feel they don't need or can't afford additional staff.

In church growth strategy, there is a rule of thumb that a minimum of one program staff person (plus backup personnel such as secretaries) should be hired for every 100 active members. Figure 4.4 shows how this rule of thumb applies to churches of varying size.

Figure 4.4

Average Attendance At Worship	Full-Time Staff Positions (minimum)
0–100	1
100–200	2
200–300	3
300–400	4
400–500	5
500–600	6
600–700	7
700–800	8

In figure 4.4, we can see that church growth necessitates a very aggressive staffing quota. Peter Wagner once advised, "investment in staff is much wiser than investment in facilities."[5]

The tri-generational approach reminds us that the task of pastoring is greater than is customarily realized. Even in small churches, there are three generations present, with different pastoral needs. The Builders in a congregation may need financial aid, daily assistance, and home visits. The Boomers may need to improve communication skills with teenage children. Generation X may need to develop vocational skills, while caring for young children.

Even when a church is too small to hire additional staff, the tri-generational approach helps a church divide duties generationally. Pastoral duties may be divided between the pastor and two or more laypersons. The Tri-Gen approach thus helps the church develop a natural division of pastoral labor.

Another characteristic that makes the smaller church awkward is its limited ability to offer more than one worship service. Schaller observes, "A second reason is that it [the awkward church] usually is too large to be able to offer a meaningful worship experience for everyone by scheduling only one service on Sunday morning, but the members often resist the idea of offering two services."[6]

Step one of the "7 Steps to a Tri-generational Church" involves viewing worship as a cultural expression of each generation, and allowing worship alternatives to develop. The hesitancy toward adding another worship service, because it hinders intimacy, can be overcome by the Tri-Gen philosophy of celebrating differences and encouraging artistic distinctiveness.

Now that we have investigated the different ideals and aspirations inherent in each of the three generations, let us consider seven steps that can lead a congregation to a healthy and growing tri-generational structure. However, keep in mind that all steps must be fully investigated and understood before any individual step is undertaken.

Part Two

7 Steps to a Tri-generational Church

Chapter Five

STEP 1: Envision Your Leadership, Church, and Community

It is one of the most difficult responsibilities conferred upon humankind. It causes more grief and vexation than any other occupation. It tears apart families, causes questioning of one's worth, and can inaugurate extended bouts of depression. It flourishes in an ever-changing state of flux, demanding new leadership skills be acquired daily. It is the utmost test of leadership, flexibility, creativity, and determination. What is this vocation that places such Herculean demands upon humankind? It is the task of parenting.

Parenting of more than one child places the parent in the difficult role of simultaneously guiding children at different stages of need, care, and understanding. While a preadolescent child craves hours of attentive encouragement, a teen of the same household will cherish increasing independence.

In addition, the parenting process is always in a state of change. It seems that as soon as one child passes through a stage, another enters it. This constant fluctuation, coupled with the difficulty of the task, makes parenting a vocation fraught with pitfalls. Little wonder the waggish Oscar Wilde observed, "children begin by loving their parents; after a time they judge them; rarely if ever do they forgive them."[1]

Envision the Tri-Gen Church as a Family

The Tri-Gen church is a congregational reflection of the family with more than one child. In this family, big brother must get along with baby brother, and toddler sis with teenage sis. It is not unusual for siblings, while young, to share a room, but as they grow, each is given his or her own space, often private bedrooms to call their own. Once children become teenagers, they usually decorate their room as a statement of individuality and personality. Though still residing within the family unit, the child has begun to make a clear statement that he or she is distinct and individual. In young adulthood, they further define their fashion, tastes, and interests. In actuality, by individualizing their ideals and aspirations they are adapting what the family believes.

A similar process unfolds when a church decides to become a tri-generational congregation. As in a home, different fashions, tastes, and interests are allowed to find their own expression and their own territory. In a family, children are allowed to listen to their own music and are given their own space (both within parameters, of course). In the Tri-Gen model, each generation is given a similar freedom to worship with their own music, and to develop classrooms, meeting areas, and worship facilities that meet their needs. However, all of this is undertaken with respect and regard for the needs and expressions of other family members.

Good parenting requires the parental leader to allow creativity and individuality, without granting *carte blanche*. So too, the leadership of a church must allow latitude, without promoting laxity. A family must decide for itself what morals it embraces, and which ideals and aspirations go against them. Likewise, each church, within the biblical convictions it holds, must decide how far each generation is allowed to go in developing individuality. Just as a family needs a final voice, the church needs leadership that encourages individuality while maintaining moral parameters.

The example of parenting can provide a starting place for

envisioning the Tri-Gen church. Many of the same dynamics are contained in both. Because most people are familiar with the dynamics of parenting, this mental picture is a springboard for our envisioning process.

Capturing a Vision Statement

Philosophy of Ministry—Mission or Vision?

Much has been written about the importance of having statements that reflect a church's philosophy of ministry, mission, and vision. As a result, there has been some confusion over what constitutes each. We embrace the idea that a *philosophy of ministry* is an extended description of the personality of a church, often seven to twenty paragraphs long. It answers the question, "Who are we, uniquely?" A *mission statement,* on the other hand, is a basic yet broad statement that answers the question "What do we do?" A *vision statement* answers the question, "Where do we believe God is calling our church to go in the future?"

Mission and vision statements are somewhat similar, and are often confused. Figure 5.1 offers a comparison of several different interpretations of *mission* and *vision.*

Figure 5.1

	George Barna[2]	Elmer L. Towns[3]	Whitesel/Hunter
Mission	A philosophic statement that undergirds the heart of your ministry.	Your ministry emphasis and your church gifting.	"What do we do?"
Vision	A clear mental image of a preferable future imparted by God, and based on an accurate understanding of God, self, and circumstances.	Same as Barna.	"Where do we believe God is calling our church to go in the future?"

Barna points out that *mission statements* are the "basic stance of the church and its intentions," thus are "broad general statements" that many churches could easily share. "To know Him and make Him known," "To reach the lost at any cost," and "To evangelize, exalt, edify and equip" are mission statements in Barna's view.[4] *Mission statements* are important, and churches should have them, but time does not permit us to address them in this book.

In addition, due to the depth and complexity of a philosophy of ministry statement, it lies beyond the scope of this present volume, as well. However, in the footnotes we have listed books that can help a church discover and describe its philosophy of ministry.[5]

Once mission and philosophy of ministry statements have been determined, a *vision* statement is necessary to direct the church toward a healthy future.

Steps to a Tri-Gen Vision Statement

A generationally inclusive *vision statement* is a crucial component in the Tri-Gen strategy. To arrive at a vision statement, the following eight steps have been adapted and expanded by the authors from ideas put forth by Elmer L. Towns.[6]

(1) Investigate the following Bible passages and glean from each characteristics of God's vision for His church: Matthew 28:18-20; John 4:21-24; Acts 2:40-47; Ephesians 4:11-16; 1 Timothy 1:5; 1 Corinthians 4:20; and Titus 2:2-8.

(2) Conduct a ministry perception questionnaire of your congregation and community.[7]

   a. Ask members open-ended questions such as, "The one thing I really like about our church is _____" and "I would really like to see us do something about _____."

b. Ask community members, "Why do you think some people in our community choose not to attend church services?" and "If you could tell the pastor of (your church name) one thing, what would that be?" (More precise recommendations for gauging the pulse and needs of your community will be covered in chapter 7.)

(3) Correlate responses to the above, and then have each member of a vision task force:
   a. Write a paragraph describing this ideal church.
   b. Edit the paragraph down to one or two lines summarizing the kind of church you think God wants you to become.

(4) Have the task force compare their results, and by consensus draft an interim vision statement.

(5) Evaluate your statement using the nine guidelines suggested by George Barna.[8] Ask yourself, is your vision statement
   • Inspiring,
   • Change oriented,
   • Challenging,
   • Empowering,
   • Long term,
   • Customized,
   • Detailed,
   • People oriented,
   • And revealing of a promising future?

(6) Rewrite the vision statement if necessary.

(7) Submit the proposed vision statement to your full leadership core for evaluation.

(8) Decide on the final wording of your vision statement.

A Sampling of Tri-Gen Vision Statements

A generationally influenced vision statement will arise in many forms. Just as families appear in a myriad of forms

109

from blended to single-parent, a tri-generational vision statement will be a distinct vision of what an individual church will look like. For many congregations with a vision statement already in place, this will only mean adding a generational component to their statement. Though this might seem an insignificant addition, the importance of keeping multigenerational thinking in the forefront of church planning and envisioning is essential for growing a Tri-Gen church.

The following are sample vision statements that have been generationally shaped to promote a Tri-Gen format.

- We want to turn pre-Christian people *of all generations* into fully devoted followers of Christ, through relevant teaching and up-to-date worship.
- We want to bring a caring and compassionate congregation that *loves people of all ages* into a relationship with Jesus Christ, through acts of kindness.
- Our vision is to *reach all generations* within the tri-state area with the good news through culture-current forms of evangelism, worship, teaching, and nurture, and to work with other congregations to accomplish these goals.
- To provide for (city) a Christian fellowship offering teaching and worship opportunities *geared to each generation*, while respecting our differences and exalting our Lord.
- The vision of (church name) is to present Christ to the people of (city) in a caring and creative way, that will *make disciples of all ages;* while offering them a forgiving and open-hearted environment.
- To *simultaneously meet the needs of all generations of people* in our community, through biblical teachings and personal lifestyle that will create social action, conscience, and responsibility.
- Our ministry goal is to *build relationships to all generations* through Christ-centered teaching, quality wor-

ship, heartfelt care, personal discipleship, and credible leadership.

- Our church vision is to become a lighthouse to the greater metropolitan area, by *addressing the needs of all generations* though parallel worship, teaching, and care ministries, which will exalt and honor our Lord Jesus Christ.

Start with Envisioning Yourself

By envisioning, we mean the ability to impart God's vision of the future of your congregation to yourself, the church leadership, the congregation, and finally, to the community. Discerning God's will for a congregation is a two-step process, first beginning with meditation upon God's Word, and continuing with a personal time of communication with God.

Dietrich Bonhoeffer, martyred German pastor, wrote in *Life Together* that "The time of meditation does not let us down into the void and abyss of loneliness; it lets us be alone with the Word. And in so doing it gives us solid ground on which to stand and clear directions as to the steps we must take."[9] Without this firm footing, all subsequent plans will be unstable and inaccurate. Meditation upon God's revealed will must be the very first activity in the envisioning process.

The Biblical Basis

Assessing God's will for his church begins with the Scriptures found in figure 5.2. Reflecting upon these Scriptures is an exercise designed to help us peer into God's biblical vision for His church.

As you undertake the exercise of figure 5.2, ask yourself what themes you see emerging. Then ask yourself, of these themes, which is the congregation already familiar with, and which are unanticipated. It is these latter, more unexpected, themes that must be considered carefully.

Figure 5.2 Read the passages below and list characteristics of God's vision for his church.

Matthew 28:18-20	John 4:21-24
1. make disciples	1. worship in spirit
2. baptize	2. " " truth
3. teach	3.

Acts 2:40-47	Ephesians 4:11-16
1. joined w/ others/met together	1. equip others to do God wk.
2. devoted to teaching & fellowship	2. each a part of the body
3. sold possessions & gave	3. mature & grow

Praise God (handwritten note in margin)

1 Timothy 1:5	1 Corinthians 4:20
1. filled w/ love	1. live by God's power
2. pure heart	2. quiet love &
3. clear conscience	3. gentleness

Titus 2:2-8
1. set good examples
2. x-generational trng.
3. accurate teaching

The Prayer Basis

In addition to biblical meditation, comes prayerful reflection. The leader that intends to discern God's direction for a congregation must spend time in pensive prayer, requesting God to reveal His will. Dietrich Bonhoeffer stressed the association between revelation and prayer when he wrote, "The Scripture meditation leads to prayer. We have already said that the most promising method of prayer is to allow oneself to be guided by the word of Scriptures...prayer means nothing else but the readiness and willingness to receive and appropriate the Word, and, what is more, to accept it in one's personal situation, particular tasks, decisions, sins, and temptations."[10] Prayer for direction is thus built upon scriptural revelation. To neglect either is to leave the first steps of the envisioning process undone.

Often, this will require setting aside an extended time for prayer, a practice that Peter Wagner observes, "is not easy for most action-oriented Americans to do. Our tendency is to get the prayer over with as soon as possible so we can get down to the 'real business.' "[11] However, in the envisioning process, prayer *is* the real business.

Prayer must also continue throughout your journey toward a Tri-Gen church. Prayer is not just an inaugural formality, but the very heart of working in partnership with a living God. Prayer not only envisions people, but it also releases God's hand to accelerate and intensify His will for a church. The following comparison by David Bryant illustrates the expeditious property of prayer.

> It may be that prayer fits into the sovereignty of God in the same way that timelapse photography makes a rose open up before my eyes in 30 seconds. If the rose hadn't unfolded naturally over a previous period of two or three days, there would be nothing on film. Similarly, as God's people unite to seek all that He has determined to do, prayer, like the movie camera, accelerates and intensifies the unfolding of all God has already willed for His Kingdom.[12]

Once a leader begins to grasp an understanding of God's preferable future for a church through Scripture and prayer, he or she must write it down. From this initial synopsis, a leader should pass along to other leaders his or her thoughts. It is among other leaders where the vision is further refined and the eight steps to a vision statement, outlined earlier in this chapter, will be employed.

Envisioning Your Leaders

Sharing robustly and energetically the vision is important to the success of the envisioning process. The Bible speaks of

God's revealed will in active, dynamic imagery. "For the word of God is living and active," declares Hebrews 4:12, "Sharper than any double-edged sword, it penetrates even to dividing soul and spirit, joints and marrow; it judges the thoughts and attitudes of the heart." In Paul's farewell to the Ephesian elders (Acts 20:32), he vividly reminds them of their future, saying, "Now I commit you to God and to the word of his grace, which can build you up and give you an inheritance among all those who are sanctified." A God-inspired vision will be dynamically shared, and enthusiastically received.

When an initial hesitancy is encountered in others, it can usually be attributed to unfamiliarity. Yet, if a vision is birthed by God, then a leader can expect support eventually. Only rarely will the leader receive a divine mandate to lead in a direction that a congregation will not willingly go. Moses' leadership of a belligerent Israel through the Sinai desert would be an example. But this is the exception, and not the rule. With the Holy Spirit active in the hearts of church leaders, eventual harmony should occur.

In most modern cases, sharing a vision imparts goal ownership, and further refines the vision. In his book, *Masterful Coaching*, management consultant Robert Hargrove observes that "shared vision is really an opportunity to create a new future that gives everyone in the organization the chance to be a part of something larger than themselves...."[13]

Diffusion theory is the technical name for how this common vision is established. But the more popular designation is the "trickle down effect." Leith Anderson, in *Dying for Change*, states that this theory diffuses new ideas downward from an upper circle of opinion makers to those who are nearer the fringes of the organization.[14] Therefore, once a leader has discerned a vision, it must be transmitted beyond the leadership core, to the staff, the volunteers, the average congregational member, and eventually (if evangelism is to result) to the community. This can be described as the trickling down of the vision to ever successive and widening groups of people (see figure 5.3).

Figure 5.3

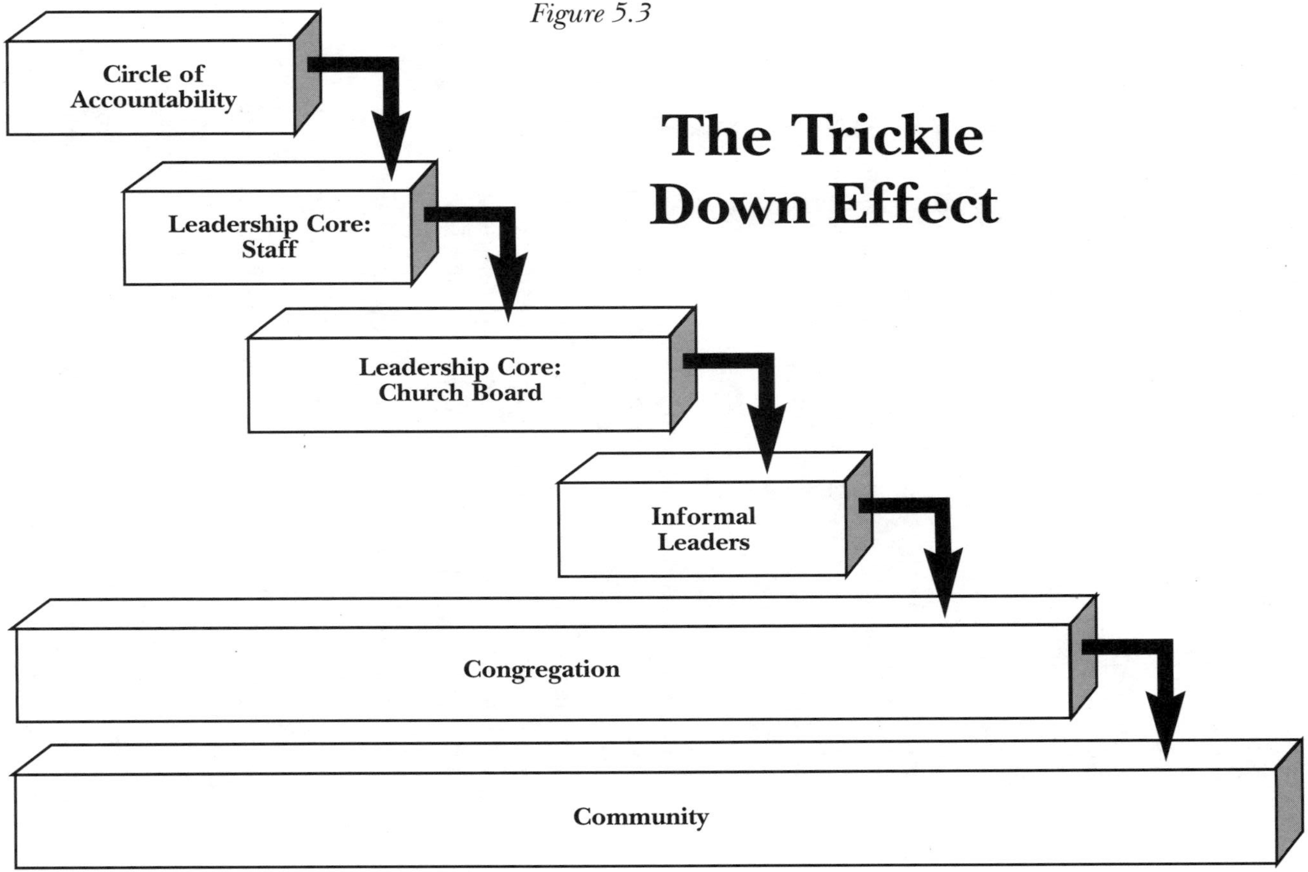

The Trickle Down Effect

Circle of Accountability

Leadership Core: Staff

Leadership Core: Church Board

Informal Leaders

Congregation

Community

As the trickle down effect takes hold, individuals become acquainted with the vision by the following progression.

A Circle of Accountability

Utilizing the trickle down effect, a leader starts by sharing the vision with a small and confidential cadre of trusted friends and colleagues. These may be key church leaders, prayer partners, professional colleagues who are not members of your church, or denominational leaders. A criterion is that they must provide a measure of accountability and perspective. The vision is further refined, by allowing godly advisors to add insights derived from Scripture and prayer. Only after the vision has been imparted to these associates should the vision be cast to wider circles.

Leadership Core: Staff

The exact process here will differ, because every church has a different leadership structure. In many churches, the second stage of the trickle down process will be to share the emerging vision with the church staff. These individuals will be greatly affected by any change in the direction of the church. In addition, their giftings and positions will make them an integral part of implementing the plan.

Leadership Core: Church Board or Council

The next group to be approached will often be a lay leadership board, administrative council, or vestry. The support of this group is key to ensuring wider distribution. In many churches, this group is elected to be a mouthpiece for the congregation. At such, it is a good barometer of congregational acceptance.

Charles Arn offers suggestions for gaining board support for new ideas. Arn suggests the following ideas be employed to attain support:[15]

- Meet with each board member individually and informally. Share your personal convictions about the idea and look to God for His will to be made known.
- Write down questions people will ask. Arn sees two types of questions here. Macro-issues relate to purpose or strategy, and might include, "Why are we doing this?" and "Is this consistent with our vision statement?" Micro-issues, on the other hand, concern details, such as, "How do we get Generation X to our church?" and "Will we have to add another service?" Arn believes it is important to address the macro-issues at this point, and leave specific micro-issues to later.
- Prepare handouts on the proposal. Handouts keep the trickle down effect on course, and give attendees something to focus upon later.

How to Trickle Down Your Vision Statement

After you have tested your emerging vision with your leadership core, it is time to go back and employ the eight steps to creating a vision statement that were outlined earlier in this chapter. In some cases, this exercise may begin with the church staff; in others, it might start with the church board, council, or vestry. In some congregations, it will begin in both groups simultaneously. Regardless, it is at this point that you want to arrive at an official vision statement.

Trickle Down the Vision to the Informal Leaders

Every congregation has opinion makers and "gatekeepers" who, though not always part of the current leadership structure, have informal veto power. Usually, they will have long-standing family ties to a congregation. In many cases, their stalwart allegiance to a church will be perceived as antiquated and obsolete. In reality, they are keepers of the history and victories of a congregation. Many of them have "pioneered" the church through its infancy and adolescence. Because of their loyalty, if they are approached privately and individually, they can become supporters. Peter Wagner, in *Leading Your Church to Growth,* states that "sometimes the pioneers can be won over, not usually by well-seasoned presentations in board meetings, but by intense one-on-one nurturing or a visitation of the Holy Spirit in genuine renewal which melts hearts and cements relationships."[16]

Our experiences have led us to believe that mistrust of new ideas also is rooted frequently in insecurity. An initial hesitancy to the Tri-Gen model often arises, because older members feel they will be forced out, or at least overlooked, when a younger generation arrives. It is here that the pastor must communicate to the Builders that the tri-generational model affords respect and honor toward each generation. The tri-generational approach assures the mature members of the congregation that their traditions, music, and programs will continue concurrently for as long as they desire. The Tri-Gen strategy is not an "either/or" proposition, but a "both/and" process.

Trickle Down the Vision to the Congregation

Once the trickle down effect has worked its way through your church leaders it is time to present it to the congregation. Here the support of the church leaders and staff can make the difference. If you have not attained the support of the church's leadership, it is not advisable to carry your vision to the congregation. If the church leadership is disregarded, then further promotion of the vision can fragment the church. George Barna warns that "if the pastor is the only individual who is promoting the vision, the church will not become a vision-driven entity."[17] Therefore, the church must experience multiple exposures to the vision from a collection of leadership voices.

Communication to the congregation can take many forms. It may include some or all of the following: sermons, teachings or homilies, topics of prayer, lessons or stories, Bible studies, special events, and guest speakers.

The last suggestion is especially helpful. A church can benefit greatly by hosting a speaker from another generation. Support for missionary endeavors historically has been built on sharing triumphs from the mission field. The purpose is to inform the church about how God is moving among members of a foreign culture. This same process can be employed in sharing what God is doing in an unfamiliar generational realm. Generational speakers can give a congregation an absorbing and eye-opening look into the move of the Holy Spirit beyond the generation gaps.

Trickle Down the Vision to the Community

The trickle down process of a tri-generational vision is not complete until it has made its way out to the community. If the Tri-Gen church is to be a wellspring of evangelism, it must communicate the good news beyond the church's perimeter. Avenues for reaching your community can include, among other things: one-on-one discussions; community involvement; caring for the homeless and disenfranchised; practicing servant evangelism; sponsorship of local events in and outside the church facility; making your facilities available to secular groups; advertisements in newspapers; television advertisements; radio ads; advertisements in phonebooks; direct mail; phone calls; news releases; and public service announcements.

In most of these approaches, a descriptive phrase or adage will be an important part of the process. Whether on a business card, a flier, or in a personal invitation, it is important to have a short phrase that describes your congregation. Too often, churches choose slogans that describe their *mission* statement. Remember, the *mission* statement is a broad general statement that can be shared by many churches.

119

Thus, if a *mission* statement is utilized, it will not serve to distinguish your individual church personality.

However, if the *vision* statement developed earlier in this chapter is used as a basis for a short description, then the intentions of the church can shine through. A vision statement may take some time to develop, but it is worth the effort. Nevertheless, it will not be as easy to remember or disseminate as a short, catchy phrase. Advertising agencies, in fact, are paid substantive amounts to create such brief mottoes, because it is easy for amateurs, in making such an abridgment, to trivialize the vision.

If your church will take the time to uncover the vision God has for your congregation, and state it succinctly, it will be a valuable tool in helping the trickle down effect reach your community.

Chapter Six

STEP 2: Leading
the Tri-generational Church

Why Is Church Leadership So Difficult?

The Difference Between Organization and Church

Why is leadership of the church so challenging? Why is the task so daunting, and the failure rate so huge? Why do most people hesitate to volunteer in an organization that runs on a volunteer basis? And why does it seem that the person who seeks to lead a flock is both admired and maligned? These are the questions that drove me to seminary. For many of my contemporaries, the purpose of seminary was to attain the licensing required by their denomination. For others, it is a way to sharpen theological and shepherding skills. For me, it had a different attraction altogether.

As a child of six, I felt a call to pastoral ministry. Although in certain teen years, that call was repressed, in college it resurfaced with an even more powerful appeal. I undeniably sensed the pastoral call, but I hesitated greatly. The difficulty pastors always seemed to encounter in managing, administrating, and leading the church troubled me. I had grown up in a large congregation, within an extended family that was heavily involved. As a result, I witnessed a spate of vilification, schisms, and second guessing. I heard leaders question the pastor's direction, administrative skill, and even sanity. If I were to succeed in my vocation, I knew I must acquire a skill for management.

With this singular frame of mind, I entered seminary. The first year was filled with the usual curriculum of theology and ministry. However, in the second year, my schedule included a class on church administration. Here came my pragmatic epiphany, for this course introduced me to the probing mind of theologian Emil Brunner. Brunner had argued in *The Misunderstanding of the Church,* that since earliest times, theologians have primarily looked at the church and seen an institution or organization.[1] When reformers such as John Calvin and Martin Luther came along, they saw the church as something more. They saw a community built on relationships, and a spiritual side that held it all together. Brunner, by describing the "hidden" or "invisible" church, helped me understand that this was very different from the church as "organization." The "invisible" or "hidden" church was the church as a "spiritual community" that existed prior to institutional forms. This spiritual community was best described by the word "church."

The "organization," with all of its administrative and bureaucratic snares, was a very different entity. In the words of one of my professors, David Luecke, "a common weakness among church leaders is a poor distinction between organization and church. Thus, what they are managing gets confused."[2] Finally, I understood the dilemma that intimidated me. I felt a sense of confidence in caring for the sheep, but had great uneasiness about managing the organization.

How this problem affects the congregation now came into clearer focus. People usually join a congregation seeking fellowship and community. When they are part of a community, their relationships are based upon respect, common interest, and reciprocal affection. However, as Kennon Callahan noticed, "They come looking for a community, and we instead put them on a committee."[3] Subsequently, when they are thrust into the organizational side of the institution, their relationships change. In the spiritual community, relations were based on need, desire, and sincerity. In

122

the institutional organization, relations are based on competence, skill, expertise—and pecking order.

The Need for Both Parallel and Unified Leadership Committees

To effectively lead the tri-generational church (or any church, for that matter), the leader must possess a clear distinction between organization and church. The church, in Luecke's words, is drawn together by "worship, learning, witnessing, and serving."[4] As a result, the church will usually manifest itself in generational sub-congregations with their own styles of worship, learning, witnessing, and serving.

Yet, the tri-generational congregation is also an organization, and this organization is comprised of three sub-congregations that will, at times, encounter common challenges. These mutual problems that face the overall organization are best addressed by unified committees. A unified committee is comprised of representatives from two or more generational sub-congregations. Parallel committees, on the other hand, are generational biased committees overseeing similar responsibilities in different generations. Figure 6.1 demonstrates these differences.

To put it another way, in the Tri-Gen church some duties will be generational specific (i.e., leading a culture-current worship service,[5] or teaching a Sunday school class), while others will be transgenerational and mutual in scope (such as caring for the facility and making major decisions about the church's future). The former are best addressed by parallel committees, the latter by unified ones.

Thus, two types of lay leader will be needed in the Tri-Gen church—organizational leaders and pastoral (church) leaders. In the tri-generational church, organizational leaders will usually sit on unified committees, made up of three generations, solving common organizational problems. But pastoral leaders who oversee worship, learning, witnessing, and

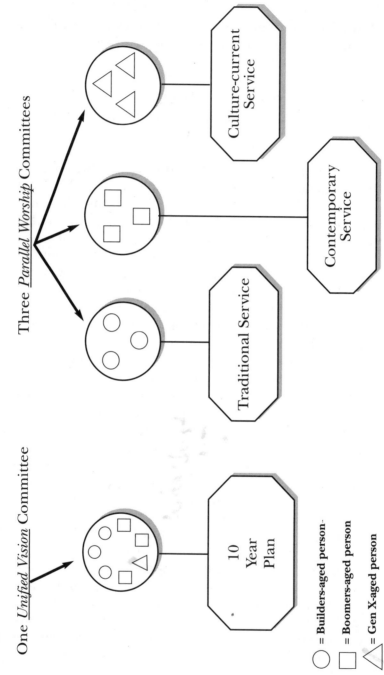

Figure 6.1

One _Unified Vision_ Committee

Three _Parallel Worship_ Committees

Culture-current Service

Contemporary Service

Traditional Service

10 Year Plan

◯ = **Builders-aged person**

☐ = **Boomers-aged person**

△ = **Gen X-aged person**

serving will function better if parallel committees arise, each having authority over their own style of worship, learning, witnessing, and serving.

The Question of Independence: Isn't Church Planting the Answer?

Donald A. McGavran once suggested that "if branches of the universal church are to obey eternal God's command, they must frequently give birth to new congregations in new segments of the population."[6] The resultant strategy was popularly called church planting, and consisted of starting new congregations. Many denominations in the 1970s and 1980s broadly and somewhat indiscriminately adopted the church planting approach to church expansion. This methodology turned out to be a highly effective and laudable strategy that has roots in the apostle Paul's method of reaching new areas.[7] In areas where there were no viable congregations, church planting was often the only way to penetrate a dissimilar culture.

But, in a society with many Christian congregations dying of geriatrophy, using the church planting approach too broadly can undercut the viability of aging congregations. The history, traditions, and triumphs of our aging congregations are valuable assets that can greatly benefit succeeding generations. Yet, McGavran is right when he says that aging churches "...frequently give birth to new congregations in new segments of the population."[8] The Tri-Gen strategy is accomplishing McGavran's goal by giving birth to new *sub*-congregations comprised of new segments of the population, *yet within the same church*. By *within the same church* we are referring to the planned birth of a sub-congregation inside the facility, leadership structure, and context of an existing congregation. Most planted churches are initially the same size as a midsized sub-congregation, where a sub-congregation is defined as from thirteen to one hundred and seventy-five people. The tri-generational approach suggests planting these sub-congregational offspring within the location, persistency, and experience of a maturing church body. This approach embraces the axiom of conservation. In addition, aging churches do not appear to have a hesitancy to do this, *if afforded some autonomy.* Those who have experienced the tri-generational model actually appreciate how relationships are maintained in the transgenerational environment.

However, not every church can or should become a tri-generational congregation. In some cases, a church planted nearby may be the most effective and unifying option for an aging church. To determine which option is best for you, we have designed a series of self-administered questions.

Figure 6.2

**Questionnaire to Determine If the
Tri-generational Format Is for You**

Circle either

1. Do younger generations make up
   15% or less of the community within
   a 12 1/2 minute drive of your church?   **Yes** or **No**

2. Is closeness and unity your highest
   priority as a church?   **Yes** or **No**

3. Are you prepared to increase by 25%
   your current level of involvement in the
   church over the next 10 years?   **Yes** or **No**

4. Are you fully prepared to eventually
   close your church?   **Yes** or **No**

5. Is your church facility in need of
   extensive structural repairs that must
   be completed in the next 5 years,
   and that total over 50% of your net
   worth?   **Yes** or **No**

If you answer "yes" to two or more of the questions in figure 6.2, questions, it is recommended that you prayerfully and carefully consider planting a daughter congregation or supporting another Tri-Gen church, before considering the Tri-Gen format for yourself. It is very likely that it is too late for the tri-generational strategy to help your congregation. Your church may be suffering from the terminal church disease described as "old age," rather than geriatrophy.

It is the authors' estimate that roughly 75 percent of the plateaued or declining churches in America will fend off demise by adopting a tri-generational approach. Once you have determined if the tri-generational approach is for you, the key to success is the autonomy you build into your leadership structure.

Leading the Tri-generational Church

Building Autonomy into Your Leadership Structure

Autonomy is important to foster creativity, tranquillity, and most important, goal ownership. In America, where the democratic ideal has pervaded our view of everything, a degree of autonomy seems necessary. The best way to build autonomy into your leadership structure, while maintaining a degree of control, is through the use of parallel committees. Parallel committees function alongside each other, each overseeing a similar function for a different sub-congregation or age group. For instance in figure 6.3, a Boomer worship committee would oversee a contemporary celebration, while a Gen-X worship committee might oversee a culture-current worship service. In addition, a Builder worship committee would supervise a traditional worship service.

Parallel committees could also be employed with Christian education, evangelism departments, and social action activities. Such structure promotes autonomy, goal ownership, and categorical thinking, while keeping intergenerational tensions to a minimum.

Avoid Headaches with Parallel Committees

"That was the last time I'll ever go to a worship committee meeting," she retorted. She was a twenty-something mother who, along with her husband, had joined the church a year before. She was known in the community as a diligent and energetic volunteer, who had helped start a community day-care. A recent congregational survey had identified her as someone who would be interested in developing a worship service that would help this Boomer and Builder church reach out to Generation X. As the consultant, I had asked her to visit the church's monthly worship committee meeting for three months and then return with her impressions.

"I can make better use of my time" was how she summed up the experience. As I inquired further, generational tension seemed to be the culprit. "The first month wasn't bad, and I didn't say much. . . . I wanted to see how it all worked. But, by the second meeting, I was ready to throw out some ideas. Well I did, and then they threw my ideas out too. . . . It was nerve wracking. . . . I got the feeling I was being attacked for things they didn't like about people my age. I understand they want young people to come to (church name), but they have a lot of hostility about it. . . . It was definitely not worth my time." Her voice was strained, and she fidgeted uncomfortably as she recounted her experience. In our previous two meetings, she had been relaxed and composed. Her physical symptoms confirmed that this had been an extremely uncomfortable experience, so I probed further. "It appears to me these meetings greatly affected you. Why do they bother you so?" "I don't want to leave this church family," she replied. ". . . I didn't know they felt that way. . . . I saw a side of them I hadn't seen before. I don't think they will ever accept people my age. . . . I wish I had never gone (to that meeting)."

As noted earlier, effective leadership requires distinguishing between organizational duties (facility management, future direction, community image) and church duties

Figure 6.3

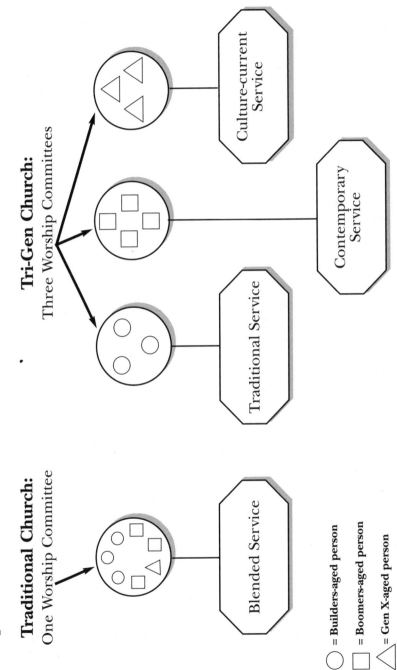

Traditional Church:
One Worship Committee

Blended Service

Tri-Gen Church:
Three Worship Committees

Traditional Service

Contemporary Service

Culture-current Service

◯ = **Builders-aged person**

▢ = **Boomers-aged person**

△ = **Gen X-aged person**

(worship, learning, witnessing, and serving). These latter tasks are best addressed by parallel committees. Parallel committees help separate the individualized ideals, values, and aspirations of each generation. They also help insulate generations from the stereotypes, frustrations, and animosities that have arisen across the generational gaps.

But, doesn't this approach require more volunteers? Of course it does, but not as many as you may expect. In the example shown in figure 6.2, seven people comprised the worship committee in the traditional church scenario. In the tri-generational option, only eleven worship committee members were needed among three parallel worship committees. This is a net requirement of only four more persons. It has been our observation that, in most churches that embrace the tri-generational approach, the addition of four people is a reasonable number.

Likewise, we have witnessed that inactive members often get re-involved when new leadership opportunities are opened up along generational lines. The reasons why people do not volunteer vary, but the underlying cause is often because people feel the cost of volunteering is not worth the benefits received. People who feel their fashion, tastes, and interests are not addressed in programming will find volunteerism difficult, if not insulting. Yet, it is not uncommon to see these inactives, who sit on the periphery of our churches, return to involvement when the exciting opportunity arises of designing worship opportunities and ministry that is customized to their fashion, tastes, and interests.

Solve Disputes with an Executive Committee

However, there must be a degree of accountability and rapport between parallel committees. There will be times when two or more parallel committees will need to have a common decision rendered. Thus, it is advisable to have so-called "oversight" or "executive committees." These committees can handle conflicts, in addition to reporting to the church leadership on behalf of the three generational biased committees.

From figure 6.3, we can now propose figure 6.4 in which an executive committee has been added not only to solve disputes, but also to report to the church administrative council or board. The executive committee is comprised of representatives of the parallel boards, who join together to form a conflict resolving and unifying oversight board.

Executive committees should include an equal number of representatives from each generationally biased parallel committee. As few as one member from each of the three parallel committees is sufficient. Even in bigger congregations, it is not advisable to let these appellate committees get too large, for here generational conflict and misunderstandings must be addressed and hammered out. Expansive size works against this process. Moreover, executive committee participants may be elected to represent their parallel committee, or designated. Participants on these executive committees should be chosen for their self -control and diplomacy. Often, it is customary to select someone with a high degree of generational bias to represent a parallel committee. It is thought that they will be a "spokesperson" for their age group. Unfortunately, this strategy can be a mistake. It is better to select those individuals who possess an ambassadorial spirit combined with an appreciation for other generations. These are the so-called "Barnabas personalities" who see the best in others, aid the misunderstood, and motivate through encouragement.

The executive committees do not add significantly to a volunteer's involvement, and may actually save time by deciding mutual issues in a smaller transgenerational environment. While a parallel board may need to meet monthly, the executive board will rarely need to meet more than every other month. Usually, executive committees will meet only quarterly, and their smaller size makes them easier to convene.

Figure 6.4

Tri-Gen Church:

- CHURCH ADMINISTRATIVE COUNCIL OR BOARD

- One Executive Committee

- Three Worship Committees

- Three Worship Services

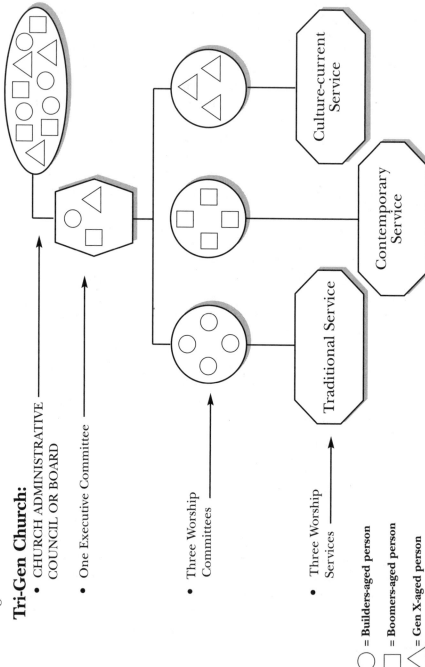

○ = **Builders-aged person**

□ = **Boomers-aged person**

△ = **Gen X-aged person**

Unify with Unified Committees

Organizational duties that address the general direction of the church, or concern the church facilities, are best handled by unified committees that are generationally balanced. Such committees will address issues that apply to an entire organization. Trustee committees that oversee the maintenance and upkeep of the facility are good examples. The preservation and refurbishment of the church buildings are a concern to all three generations. The Boomer will want to ensure that the facilities are updated and professional looking, while the Builder will wish to guarantee that they retain their historical spirit and expression. The Gen-Xer will want the facility to offer adequate childcare areas, places for small group interaction, and up-to-date technology.

How to Divide Your Committees

Parallel Committees

The following examples are church tasks that lend themselves to parallel committees. Though the designations may vary from church to church and among different traditions, the character of each committee is what is being described. It is helpful to remember that parallel committees (and their executive committees) generally oversee areas of worship, learning, witnessing, and serving.

Some parallel committee examples might include worship; Christian education and Sunday school; small groups; evangelism; congregational care and lay shepherding; social action and social welfare; local or home mission; choirs and music teams; ushers and greeters; communion; newcomer follow-up committees; self-help groups; deacons (in terms of their role of serving); men's ministries; and women's ministries.

Unified Committees

The following are examples of church tasks that often best lend themselves to unified committees. Again, the names may change among different traditions, but the general idea of each committee should be clear. Examples include: board of trustees; administrative council or church governing board; staff/parish relations committees or personnel committees; nominating committees; finance and audit committees; membership, baptism and confirmation committees; foreign mission committees; stewardship committees; funeral/memorial committees; vision and long-range planning committees; liaison committees to denominational organizations; delegates to district and national conferences; church-wide publication, bulletin and newsletter committees; church-wide event committees, where the event is designed to attract all three generations; and committees charged with promoting unity building events in the church.

These lists are not intended to be definitive, but rather to give an idea of the type of committee that falls within each area. In every church situation the committees, boards, teams, and vestries will take on their own unique personality. Therefore, utilize the above as general guidelines rather than as definitive lists.

Generational Ratios for Your Committees

Sometimes, the question arises as to the optimum generational ratio for unified committees. Should a unified committee be made up of equal numbers of Builders, Boomers, and Generation X? Or should the ratios reflect the percentage of Builders, Boomers, and Generation X already in a congregation? The preferred strategy for unified committees is to employ generational ratios that mirror the community makeup, rather than the congregation. If a unified committee has a generational balance that reflects the community, then the church will proceed in directions that are more in step with the community. A community generational ratio can make the church more relevant to the community outside the church's walls.

However, in many congregations it is difficult to staff your committees with community generational ratios, when you are lacking certain age groups. In this case, the next best scenario is to staff your unified committees with a ratio that reflects your congregational makeup, provided you have at least some representation from each age group. A simple congregational questionnaire can be administered to check the generational ratios of your church. Remember to ask for the year of birth and not the age, since the latter changes yearly and can lead to confusion later. Figure 6.5 is an example of how this question can be asked.

Figure 6.5

WHEN WERE YOU BORN?			
Before 1946	**1946–1964**	**1965–1983**	**1984–2002**

Staffing the Tri-generational Church

When You Don't Want a Youth Pastor

In the church, adding staff seems to follow a predictable pattern. In small churches, the professional pastoral staff will usually consist of one pastor. This pastor will be responsible for training, preaching, counseling, initiating outreach, and organizing worship. A paid secretary or office worker will sometimes be included. At this point, the pastor is the primary inspiring figure and leader. A church will usually plateau at around ninety people in Sunday attendance at this stage, unless the pastor uses his or her skills to train laypeople to assist in the work of ministry.

As the church grows and laity are involved, a second professional shepherd is hired. Often, this will be a music minister/director, a Christian education director, or a youth pastor/leader. In each tradition, the terminology, as well as the position, may vary. But, across the board, among varying denominations, the most customary option is the hiring of a youth pastor/leader.

Often, this course is taken because of growing concern among congregational leaders about the generation gaps that are separating them from their teenage offspring. Once a few vocal members of a church board have teenagers, the call for a professional youth worker becomes deafening. Yet, hiring a youth worker may be not only a disservice to your children, but an injustice to the youth pastor, as well.

Why You Don't Want a Youth Pastor

The number of people was far beyond what I had expected. The line was at least twenty feet long, and it would be more than an hour before I would leave the auditorium. I had just finished addressing approximately four hundred youth pastors at the National Youth Workers Convention in St. Louis. "You are talking about where I am at," blurted out a blond-haired young man sporting two ear piercings and a tie-dyed shirt. A little later, another young man would say, "If I could do it, I might stay in the ministry." Still later, a middle-aged woman shared, "If I had looked at ministry that way, I'd be happier right now." What was it from the afternoon lecture that resonated so clearly with the youth workers assembled? It was a description of the tri-generational church and a seminar title: "The Late Great Youth Leader."

My premise was that the youth leader was an inadequate solution to the problem of youthful angst. In addition, the youth leader or pastor, as typically utilized, is a misappropriation of person power. Let me explain. The youth leader usually is given shepherding responsibilities of young people in their teens. Most youth leaders are given authority over children in middle school through high school. Some programs will give them responsibility for those a bit younger, and others will give them responsibility that includes those a bit older. But the age range for their oversight is roughly a seven to ten year span of time. The youth leader's job description often resembles that of a pastor, only relegated to a more finite age span. He or she has responsibilities over youth worship, learning, witnessing, and serving. In essence, the youth leader is a mirror of the pastor, only on a smaller scale. Church leaders perceive that lifelong attitudes about religion will be germinated during the teen years—and they are right.

But, one problem arises—the youth leader's energy is limited to a rather small and confined age range. Remember, the youth leader expends pastoral energies over an age span of seven to ten years. We wouldn't think of doing this with any other age group. We probably wouldn't hire a pastor to minister to people from age 40 to 47, or from age 50 to 60. We expect our pastors to shepherd a wider age range. Many senior pastors shepherd several generations, not only simultaneously, but remarkably well. Limiting associate pastors to congregants born in a seven to ten year span of time is probably squandering our pastoral talent.

Granted, a part-time youth pastor may need to restrict the range of his or her pastoral oversight. But, in congregations that can afford a full-time youth worker, limiting the pastoral supervision to such a small range is ill advised. The Tri-Gen approach does not advocate that one person try to pastor all ages and all generations, but our approach does believe that a seven to ten year age span for pastoral responsibility is too restrictive. Teens are certainly asking grand metaphysical questions during these years, but aren't adults also facing such questions when marriages dissolve, loved ones die, and they are facing their own death? Teen years are truly years that require careful pastoral guidance, but do we misappropriate our person power, when we limit the second pastor we hire to such a small range of congregants?

A second quandary is that the youth leader often feels

stuck in an adolescent ministry. As his or her charges mature and pass on to adulthood, the youth leader finds himself or herself left behind, increasingly being identified as a perpetual teenager. One youth leader referred to himself as "the Dick Clark of First Baptist." He went on to protest, "... my advice is never really taken (by the church leadership) because in everyone's eyes I'm always a teenager." Later he predicted, "I have no chance of becoming a pastor unless I go to another church."

Don't Focus Too Narrowly When Staffing

A better strategy than hiring a youth leader/pastor as your second professional ministry position, is to hire a "generational pastor." By this, we mean a pastor who is given responsibility for a generational span of approximately 19 years. A Generation X pastor might be given responsibility for congregants born between 1965 and 1983. In 2001, these would be congregants between the ages of 18 to 36. A Boomer might pastor those born between 1946 and 1964, who would be aged 27 to 55 in 2001. A Builder might pastor those born in 1945 and before, which would be 56 and above in 2001. A Generation Y pastor might pastor children ages 17 and under, born between 1984 and 2002. Figure 6.6 gives a graphical view of how a generational staffing model might look if financial resources and personnel were available.

On the surface, this looks like a very aggressive staffing agenda. But it is not suggested that these generational pastors be put in place all at once, or even that they need to be. Some pastors are gifted at pastoring more than one generation, and in the smaller church, this may be necessary. But, generational staffing should be followed as growth occurs and monies become available.

For instance, it may be easier for a Boomer pastor to oversee the Builders also, at least initially (see figure 6.7). If a second pastor is to be added, it might be prudent to add a

Generation X pastor. After that, it may be wise to add a Gen-Y pastor or a Builder pastor, depending on the need.

Many churches are discovering the value of adding a Builder pastor who can allocate the time needed for home visitation of an increasingly immobile generation. This can often be a good fit for a semi-retired pastor in the community. Such opportunities allow aging ministers to keep active with viable ministry long after the age where they have enough energy to oversee a multigenerational church.

Figure 6.6

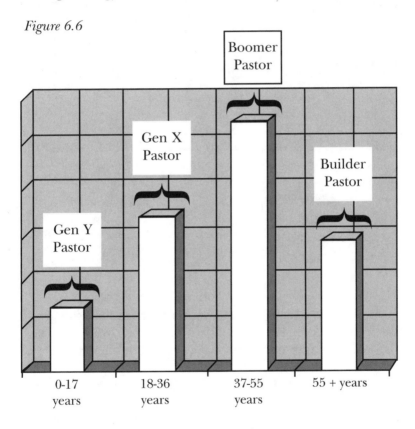

Figure 6.7, gives an example of how a congregation's generational ratio can be partitioned into two pastoral zones.

139

Figure 6.7

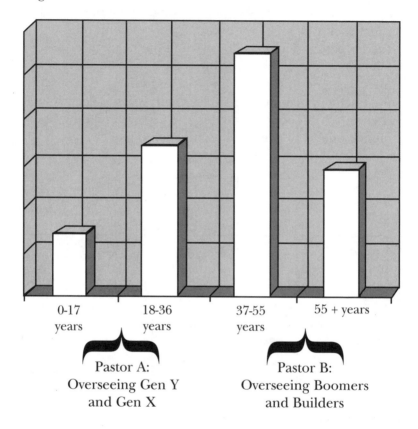

With proper planning, the church in figure 6.7 can grow with a balanced generational structure that will eventually allow the addition of more generational shepherds, as seen in figure 6.8.

The generational approach to staffing has several reasons to commend it, including the following.

Clearly defined pastoral ranges. A generational pastor has a clearly defined age range to shepherd. The generational pastor knows whom he or she is responsible for, and there is less likelihood of individuals falling through the cracks.

Figure 6.8

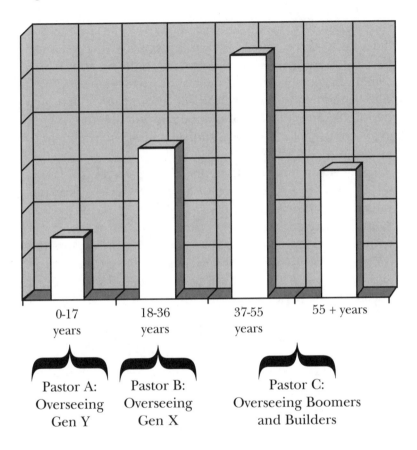

0-17
years

18-36
years

37-55
years

55 + years

Pastor A:
Overseeing
Gen Y

Pastor B:
Overseeing
Gen X

Pastor C:
Overseeing Boomers
and Builders

Consistency in ministry. The generational staffing strategy ensures consistency in ministry. Rather than leaving
parishioners after they have reached a certain age, a generational pastor continues to shepherd them as they age. For
instance, when a young person enters the mid-twenties, the
typical youth pastor will relinquish control. At this point,
many young people encounter a sense of vulnerability and
abandonment. The youth pastor with whom they have grown

up is now tending a flock of new adolescents. Because the senior pastor has delegated oversight of the youth to the youth pastor, the twenty-something person may not feel sufficiently linked to the senior shepherd. At this juncture, because there is no clear pastoral oversight for the twenty-something person, a great deal of departure often occurs. The generational staffing approach allows the generational pastor to continue to shepherd the person indefinitely. They grow up in Christ together, and they have the potential to grow old together.

Longevity in ministry. Over and over again youth workers tell us they are engaged in youth work because it is a stepping stone to the pastoral ministry. Youth work for many is a rite of passage, where a budding pastor earns his or her stripes. However, when youth leaders feel it is time to move up, they must usually pry themselves away from their sheep and start fresh elsewhere. In the generational staffing approach, the pastor ages along with his or her parishioners. Thus, a leader can eventually become a pastor of adults without ever being forced to leave a congregation he or she has invested time and treasure into. In such environments, associate pastors are usually happier, more fulfilled, and more hopeful.

Team teaching. Bill Hybels said that "one of Willow Creek's most helpful contributions to the contemporary church has been team teaching."[9] Hybels, pastor of the large Willow Creek megachurch in South Barrington Illinois, sees the team teaching concept as not only rescuing senior pastors from self-destructive schedules, but allowing the congregation to hear God's voice through multiple speakers. A generational staffing approach naturally fosters this by allowing generational pastors to preach at different generational worship expressions; or, by rotating speakers among different worship expressions on a monthly, quarterly or weekly basis. Whichever of these approaches is chosen, it is important to have a unified stance on truth and doctrine;

while allowing the delivery, style, and spirit of the sermons to vary to a predetermined degree.

With the above understandings and ideas in place, it is now fitting to move to Step 3, where we shall look beyond the church's walls to study the unchurched of your community, and identify their needs.

Chapter Seven

STEP 3: Identify the Needs of the Unchurched

Identifying and addressing the needs of others is a theme that tenaciously runs throughout the Scriptures. In Moses' upper desert discourse, the 120-year-old leader commands Israel "... to be openhanded toward your brothers and toward the poor and needy in your land" (Deuteronomy 15:11). He sought to remind a generation destined to possess the land that obeying God's laws toward brother and alien alike brought success and abundance. In addition, he stressed that disobedience brought unavoidable consequences.

In the Kingdom Period, meeting the needs of others was a praiseworthy attribute. King Lemuel's mother suggested to her son that "a wife of noble character who can find?" (Proverbs 31:10*a*). Though difficult to discover, such a woman would nonetheless be a spouse who "extends her hand to the needy" (31:20*b*).

In New Testament times, Paul would prescribe benevolence toward the needy as the cure for selfishness and larceny. Paul required that a person caught stealing would be accountable to do "something useful with his own hand, that he may have something to share with those in need" (Ephesians 4:28 *c,d*). Clearly, addressing the needs of others was the remedy for, and possibly inoculation against, selfishness. A corollary that might be inferred from this is that keeping the needs of the unchurched before the congregation prevents navel-gazing, and at worst, disregard.

A Place to Start: Which Churches Nearby Are Growing?

The term "felt needs" is a colloquialism that refers to those needs that are most acutely and fundamentally felt by a person and/or segment of the population. The first step in identifying and addressing the needs of unchurched people begins with observing which churches in close proximity are growing. In *Frontiers in Missionary Strategy*, Peter Wagner describes this as an anticipatory strategy, observing, "Wherever some churches are actually growing among a certain people, others probably can grow there also."[1] If a congregation is lacking in Generation X members, then an examination of those churches in the area that are reaching this generation will be a helpful first step. The same is true if a congregation is missing Boomers or Builders.

In our consulting work, we have found that growing churches often possess less territorialness than plateaued churches. These expanding churches are often delighted to offer a struggling congregation ideas, data, and strategies that will assist in outreach.

Caution must be exercised here to draw a distinction between reproducible patterns of growth and those based on factors that cannot be duplicated, such as unusually gifted pastors. Donald A. McGavran admonished in *Understanding Church Growth* that "research should look for *reproducible patterns of growth* possible to ordinary congregations, ordinary pastors, and ordinary missionaries" (italics McGavran).[2] Figure 7.1 offers questions designed to uncover reproducible strategies and can serve as the basis for an interview with a growing church's leadership.

However, if there are no churches in the area reaching the generation(s) missing in your church, caution should be exercised. This situation could be caused wholly by the lack of a church that is addressing the missing needs. However, it could also be because of an absence of these generations in the community. Assessing the U.S. Census data discussed later in this chapter will be helpful in answering this question. Yet, whatever the outcome, looking for reproducible patterns in other churches is a fundamental starting place in uncovering felt needs and ministries that fulfill them.

Figure 7.1

Questions to Ask Growing Churches
That Are Reaching Generations You Are Seeking to Attract

1. What ages (or generations) are growing in number within your congregation?
2. What programs/ministries do you feel are most effective in reaching these ages?
3. When did you begin employing these ministries?
4. How long did it take before these ministries were successful, in your opinion?
5. How many people did it take to start each ministry?
6. How many people does it take to effectively maintain each ministry?[3]
7. What type of person(s) is/are necessary to maintain this strategy?
8. Did you use any published strategy, book, consultant, or ministry tools?
9. Would you consider sharing these tools with our church, or telling us where we could acquire them ourselves?

Probing Deeper: Census Data

The United States Census Bureau offers an abundance of data on population size, demographic distribution, economic makeup, social characteristics, and generational ratios. An analysis of this data is the next step in ascertaining the needs of unchurched people living nearby.

Census data is available in printed form at most public and college libraries. Library personnel can be of great help in sifting through its many volumes.

One of the most accessible and manageable formats for census data can be found on the World Wide Web. The United States Census Bureau Web site offers a searchable database that can help you select data for your community in seconds.

What Information Are You Looking For?

Collecting and collating information from either a library or the World Wide Web requires foresight and planning. To conduct successful research consider the following.

First, determine the size of the area you wish to examine. Typically, an unchurched person can be expected to travel up to twelve and a half minutes to regularly attend church services. However, in some areas this range varies. In some cities, travel time will increase to thirty-five minutes. In other municipalities, it may decrease. In our experience, residents of Los Angeles will travel further to church than those of Chicago or New York. In addition, rural residents often will drive longer distances. In mountainous areas and/or terrain dotted by small lakes, marshes, and other natural impediments, travel time will drop to fifteen minutes. One way to determine the distance potential visitors will drive to your church is to undertake these three steps.

(1)   Look up in the United States Census data the distances people drive to and from work in your community. A rule-of-thumb is that people will drive on average 60 percent of this distance to church. Compute this percent.

(2)   Next, poll members of the church who have joined in the past two years. It is best to poll only formerly unchurched people. However, the small number of these people in some churches may necessitate polling all newcomers. Regardless of the con-

stituency sampled, find out the distances they drive to church. Here again, compute the average.

(3) Finally, correlate these findings by adding together the averages and multiply by .60 (60 percent). This yields a figure that is weighted toward the longer distance, usually the distance people in your community drive to work. Because new members to your congregation most likely have come because of a friend's invitation, the distance they drive may be overly influenced by your existing congregational members. Adding the two averages attained in steps 1 and 2 above, and then multiplying by .60, will yield a more realistic number.

The next step in conducting a successful search is to decide whether you want to look at the census data by postal code (zip code) or specific census area (called "State-County-Census Tract" by the Census Bureau). Zip codes were designed to aid the U.S. Postal Service in ease of delivery, and often change in growing areas. Though they can be the easier to attain, they may not be as reliable as looking at census areas or "tracts." Tracts are divided into states, counties, and cities. Figure 7.2 offers some hints on when to use each method.

Figure 7.2

When to Use the Census Tract Method

Use this method if your congregation is situated within a small to midsize town or city, where a 20 minute drive would roughly cover an entire city, community, or town.

When to Use the Zip Code Method

If your church is in a large city, you may find zip codes better encompass the area you wish to analyze. Rural communities with one or more small towns nearby will also find the zip code method of data gathering more beneficial.

Do not be intimidated by the wealth of census data available. Tables from the Census Bureau cover 300 variables including race, household type, presence of children, home values, age, and so forth. Take some time and peruse the various tables of data. McGavran cautioned in *Understanding Church Growth* that with census data, "you will have to pan tons of gravel to get an ounce of gold."[4] But, what gold it will be! Census data will allow your congregation to discreetly analyze the lifestyles and social patterns of your unchurched neighbors.

Do not forget to check whether you are looking at the latest data. Much of the information available at libraries will be 1990 data, at least until late in the year 2001 (earlier via the Internet). Even after 2001, the 1990 data will be more accessible for a time. Do not entirely ignore older data, for it will be helpful in interpreting the past and charting future trends. However, because a revision of census data is taking place, be careful to check which data you are using.

Finally, read the definitions published by the Census Bureau. Controversy was generated during earlier census gatherings over the ethnic labels the government employed. The Census Bureau has tried to clarify and improve these categories. Thus, because cultural terminology is always in a state of flux, it is important to understand the definitions used for the specific census you are studying.

How to Get Census Data from the Web

Attaining census data from the World Wide Web is the easiest and most accurate method of data collection. Five short steps are required to glean the appropriate data.

(1) Point your Internet browser to the home page for the United States Census Bureau at http://www.census.gov. Click on the "search" button.

(2) On the next page, choose "Place Search." Type in the zip code or the name of the place for which you wish demographic information.

(3) On the following "U.S. Gazetteer" page click on either table STF3B (if using the zip code method), or STF1A or STF3A (if using the place method). Make a note of the table you are using for reference purposes.

(4) Place a "check" next to the data tables from which you wish information. Since this is a long list of over 300 variables, it is wise to experiment until you obtain the data you need.

(5) Click "submit." Next you will be asked to "Choose Data Option Retrieval Method." This is a formatting option. Clicking the default "HTML" button will usually produce the most readable format. In seconds, you will see the demographic data you requested on your screen. On most computers and Internet terminals you can then print the results.

Other Sources of Census Data

Many denominational agencies and judicatories offer census data and demographic studies at low to no cost. In addition, a number of private companies offer marketing reports based upon census data. Though the cost may be substantial, these professionally prepared demographic studies can be very useful.

The Task Force—Help for the Church on a Limited Budget

For the church on a limited budget, following the guidelines of this chapter will assist in assembling census data readily, quickly, and inexpensively. The greatest cost will be in time and person power. Therefore, the best approach is to delegate to a sub-committee or task force the responsibility of researching and depicting the felt needs of the generations missing from your congregation. It is also important to attach a time limit to the goal of collecting data. Usually, within a thirty to sixty day span of time, a committee or team can adequately research and analyze census data.

Assessing Felt Needs from Census Data

From census data, it is relatively easy to identify the basic needs of people in a reachable proximity. If there is an abundance of single people, then ministries that address such persons will meet felt needs. If the community is experiencing an influx of married couples with children under eighteen years of age, then ministries geared toward parents of school-aged children will be advantageous. And if your community has a profusion of "female householders" with "no husband present" and "children under 18," then ministry to single mothers will be needed. Assessing *basic* needs from census data is straightforward and self-evident. However, to ascertain *deeper* felt needs it is important to probe beneath the superficial questions of a census toward heart-felt needs. Focus groups and community surveys will be the next steps in this process.

The Power of Focus Groups

Focus Group Basics

Focus groups have been used by psychological researchers to bring to the surface feelings that might remain buried in one-on-one interviews. In the group context, people will often build upon one another's responses to reveal more about their inner feelings and convictions. A focus group can be a helpful tool for bringing to the surface the needs of a community.

Where did it get its name? A focus group helps an organization "focus" on which information is relevant by analyzing a group response to a question or series of questions.

How many people make up a focus group? The focus group

method succeeds because it fosters the intimacy and candor of the cell or primary group described in chapter 1. A cell group is typically three to twelve people, and so is the focus group.

How to Conduct a Focus Group

A focus group should only be conducted with absolute integrity, honesty, and professionalism. Because of this, many churches choose to have a professional firm conduct such assessments. However, if certain guidelines are followed, a church can successfully conduct its own focus group exercise. The following are guidelines that must be considered.

Group composition. Because felt needs are personal in nature, it is best it utilize nonattendees who are neighbors, coworkers, or friends of existing members, and focus groups yield the best data when they are composed of like-aged people.[5] Focus group participants should also be from the generation you are targeting. Before they participate, they should have their questions answered as well as being appraised of the guidelines contained in the figure 7.3 checklist.

Figure 7.3

Focus Group Participant Checklist

A. We will be hosting a focus group of 3 to 12 people who will be asked to reflect on what people your age are looking for in a church. This will be done in an informal and relaxed manner, but will be very helpful to our church. Are you interested in being a part of this group?   ❏ yes   ❏ no

B. This meeting will be recorded.
May we record it on videotape?   ❏ yes   ❏ no
May we record it on audiotape?   ❏ yes   ❏ no

C. May we use your name?   ❏ yes   ❏ no

D. The location will be ____(fill in location here)____.

E. The meeting will begin at _____ and conclude by _____.
Please note. Though you will not be paid for participation, you will greatly help our church understand what people such as yourself are looking for in a church. Thank you.

Group location. A neutral venue is preferred. Libraries, city halls, schools, offices, and even marketing firms have been used. The site should be intimate and private. Often congregations are tempted to use the church facility. However, church buildings can unduly influence a focus group participant (either positively or negatively).

Meeting setup. It is important to have comfortable chairs and a relaxing environment. The meeting should be recorded on an audiocassette or videotape. Due to the potential controversial nature of some responses, most focus groups prefer the anonymity of audio recording. In either circumstance, it is also important to record the proceedings in written form to engender analysis and reevaluation.

A moderator is essential. The moderator should not only be a person closely acquainted with the goals of the meeting, but one who also demonstrates a desire to identify the needs of the target generation. The person chosen should understand the tasks of a moderator as outlined in figure 7.4.

Figure 7.4

The Tasks of a Focus Group Moderator

A. Put the focus group participants at ease.

B. Implement the focus group agenda.

C. Steer the group away from controversial topics and injurious remarks.

D. Tactfully elicit comments from less verbal members.

E. Keep the discussion on track.

Meeting structure. Figure 7.5 introduces a suggested format for a focus group meeting.

Figure 7.5 A Suggested Focus Group Agenda

Introductions

Moderator: Let me introduce myself...

Moderator: Let us go around the room and have each person introduce him or her self...

Participants: (introduce themselves).

Moderator: The purpose of our focus group is to discover what people your age are looking for in a church. Your advice will be very helpful to us. In addition, the meeting will conclude promptly at _____.

Moderator: May I record our meeting on videotape or audiotape for future reference?

Moderator: (add any other policies or announcements here).

Data Gathering

Moderator: Why do you think some people in your age group choose not to attend church services?

Participants: (respond)

Moderator: What do you perceive as the needs of people your age?

Participants: (respond).

Moderator: What are the needs of people your age that a church can best address?

Participants: (respond)

Moderator: If you could tell the pastor of   *(your church name)*   one thing, what would that be?

Participants: (respond)

Close the meeting with acknowledgment and gratitude.

SOME DOS AND DON'TS FOR MODERATORS OF FOCUS GROUPS

Do

Make everyone feel comfortable.

Keep the meeting on track.

Encourage quiet attendees to speak up.

Stick to your key questions, either those from figure 7.5, or others designed for your situation.

End on time.

Don't

Let a few participants monopolize the conversation.

Be surprised or frustrated by unexpected or aggressive comments.

Try to defend or answer any comments. Let the natural conversation flow unimpeded by your own opinions.

Forget to set a time limit for the meeting. Focus group meetings typically last one to one-and-a-half hours.

The Benefits of Focus Groups

Focus groups harness the intimacy and openness of the cell group dynamic, allowing people to share buried feelings. When assessing felt needs, it is critical to probe beneath the surface to uncover recessed hurts, suspicions, and desires. In addition, the proper utilization of focus groups can be a cathartic event for the congregation, as well as for participants.

One-on-One Interviews

Written, Door-to-Door, or Phone Interviews?

A questionnaire or survey with open-ended responses is another good method for discovering felt needs. In this approach, a question is asked that begs an extended written or verbal response.

However, many people do not make the effort to complete printed questionnaires that require written responses. Thus, surveys that are administered verbally by a facilitator and to which only a verbal response is required have a higher acceptance ratio. It is more likely that a respondent will reply, when the facilitator is doing the writing rather than the other way around. Because of this, surveys are usually more productive when conducted as a one-on-one interview. Two of the most popular formats for a one-on-one interview are the door-to-door visit and the phone interview.

The door-to-door interview was a popular survey method in the 1950s and 1960s. Groups such as Campus Crusade for Christ witnessed many conversions as a result of this canvassing method. Many church members will remember the success of such models and wish to repeat them.

Today, however, the telephone is a less obtrusive (but not completely unobtrusive) method of conducting a one-on-one interview. Due to the rise in crime and the quest for privacy, many people resent the intrusion of a doorway visit. The phone interview allows the respondent a degree of autonomy and privacy.

However, marketers for everything from phone services to mutual funds have discovered the power of the phone interview. Therefore, it is recommended that a phone interview be conducted carefully and within the guidelines listed in figure 7.6.

To ensure the accuracy and veracity of the telephone survey, it is important that the interviewer understand the following principles that are involved in figure 7.6 questions.

Question #1. It is often too confrontational to ask "What is your greatest need?" Therefore, this question asks about general needs of the age group, yet the answer will often reflect the person's personal felt needs.

Question #2. This question helps the interviewer understand why the respondent and/or their friends have not become an active participant in a church. It is important for the interviewer not to become defensive or judgmental. Actively listen and withhold all commentary, regardless of how tempting the initiation of an apologetic retort.

Figure 7.6 Telephone Need Assessment Survey

Introduction

"Hello. My name is ___(name)___ and I am conducting a short survey for ___(name of congregation)___ in ___(city/town)___. Would you mind if I asked you a few anonymous and short questions?"
  * If "YES" continue.
  * If "NO" conclude by saying. "Thank you for your consideration, good-bye."

Survey Parameters

"We wish to interview individuals who were born in the years ___(year)___ to ___(year)___.[5] Were you born in or during these years?
  * If "YES" continue.
  * If "NO" conclude by saying "Thank you for your time, good-bye."

Open-ended Questions

Question #1: "What do you think a church could do to help people aged _____ to _____?"

Question #2: "Why do you think people aged _____ to _____ do not attend church services?"

Question #3: "What are people your age looking for in a church?"

Question #4: "What advice could you give me so that a church could help people age _____ to _____ more effectively?"

Question #5: "Are you currently actively involved in a church, synagogue, mosque, or other religious house of worship?"

Conclusion

Thank you for your time. Your advice will help ___(name of___ ___congregation)___ of ___(city/town)___ better address the needs of people in our community(ies). Thank you. Good-bye.

Question #3. This question will identify the respondent's view of effective church ministry toward people like oneself. But, if your church is small, you will not be able to meet all the needs identified by your respondents. Focus on two to five needs, depending on your size, which you feel your church can address.

Question #4. This question may come as a surprise to your respondent, since most people think of Christians as people who tell others what to do. This question initiates a loving, caring, and concerned interest toward the respondent. It is critical that this concern be genuine. Any feigned or fabricated concern is usually discernible by the interviewee.

Question #5. Ask this question only if the interview has proceeded congenially. The purpose of this question is to determine if the interviewee is actively involved in a religious community. If the interview has contained elements of stress and/or tension, the interview may be perceived as a covert enticement to membership. Under such circumstances, it is better not to ask Question 6. Always keep in mind that the goal of a need assessment survey is to establish needs, not to proselytize.

How Many Phone Interviews Are Needed?

Demographers and experimental psychologists have found that random samples of 1,500 people can provide a remarkably accurate snapshot of the opinions of a community and even a whole nation.[6] However, the magnitude of such a survey will be beyond many congregations (but not all). In addition, many professional companies can conduct these services.[7]

However, congregations can attain usable results from a small sample, especially when a smaller community is involved. The rule of thumb is to attempt to sample 1 percent of the target population. If, according to census data, 30,000 Baby Boomers live within a twenty-minute drive of your congregation, a good sample would be 300 completed phone calls. This may seem an immense size, but it can be easily sampled over a four week period with a handful of volunteers. Interviewers should expect calls to last approximately 5 to 15 minutes. The best and most unobtrusive times to call are listed in figure 7.7.[8]

Figure 7.7

> **When Are the Best Times to Conduct Telephone Surveys?**
>
> Evenings between 6:30 and 9 P.M.
>
> Saturdays from 10 A.M. to 4 P.M.
>
> Sundays from noon to 9 P.M.

[handwritten: X s/ use cellphones]

[handwritten: why not at 10-12 when people aren't in church?]

Correlating Responses to Needs: A Three Part Process

Part 1. Immediately after concluding each phase of the survey process, the individuals who conduct each component should rank in order the needs they perceive. It is important to undertake this exercise immediately after the focus group meeting or phone interview when memory is lucid and fresh.

Part 2. Next, have each interviewer compose a list of programming and ministry ideas that could address the needs one has witnessed. Utilizing a structure like figure 7.8 can be helpful.

Part 3. Convene a meeting of all interviewers to correlate their responses. Break into groups of from three to seven participants. Then answer the following:

Can common needs be identified by the responses?

Are common ministries and/or programs available to meet those needs? With your group, categorize and prioritize both the needs and ministries you identified.

Share these lists with both the leadership core and the senior leader.

Figure 7.8

Need:	Ministry:
Child care for working mothers of preschool aged children	Daycare provided by the church. Carpooling service for preschools in the area Have the youth group organize child care on Saturday morning so parents can do their grocery shopping or spend time with each other. Serve a breakfast for mothers with preschool children once a week from 6 to 8 A.M. Staff it with stay at home mothers or Builders.
After school care for school age children	Kid's Club provided by church after school day ends Join with other community churches providing after school recreational activities. Start an after school choir called "Praise Kids."

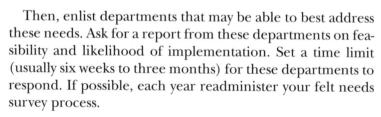

Then, enlist departments that may be able to best address these needs. Ask for a report from these departments on feasibility and likelihood of implementation. Set a time limit (usually six weeks to three months) for these departments to respond. If possible, each year readminister your felt needs survey process.

Chapter Eight

STEP 4: Worship in a Tri-generational Format

Indigenous Worship Celebrations

Combating Cultural Overhang

In seminary, there are times when some new understanding or insight suddenly releases comprehension where once there was confusion. These unanticipated interludes are infrequent, but invaluable. One such epiphany for me occurred at Fuller Seminary while I was digesting *Frontiers in Missionary Strategy* by Peter Wagner.

Wagner warned of a "present and potentially dangerous" barrier to effective ministry, which he labeled "cultural overhang."[1] Cultural overhang occurs when one culture's preferences and affinities subtly overhang or protrude into another culture. Christians unconsciously embrace cultural overhang because, according to Wagner, "no one who moves to a second culture is able to shed his old skin completely. Deep in the heart of man, even in missionaries, lurks that 'creator complex' by which he delights in making other people over in his own image."[2]

Unwittingly letting our own cultural preferences overhang and intrude into a different indigenous culture is subtle, invasive, and pervasive. For example, missionaries to South Africa once required native Africans to learn

European languages, before they could be taught the gospel. The result of cultural overhang is that we expect an indigenous culture to embrace our culture, before they can respond to the good news. Often, the indigenous culture never truly—nor widely—embraces the good news, because it is cloaked in a different cultural attire.

Cultural overhang in the church can be seen in the conflict that arises over musical tastes and instrumentation. People of different cultures listen to different musical instruments, which make different sounds. The musical sounds one culture grows up being familiar with may be alien (or at least, outdated) to another culture. African melody is highly rhythmic in nature, relying on the deep tones and staccato beats of instruments indigenous to the African continent. European music was characterized by linking music and technology, giving rise to the technological advancement of the pipe organ, followed by the harpsichord, and the piano.

As a result of these different beginnings, African music produced the zest and festivity of the African American spiritual, while European tastes dictated the stately and melodically technical masses of Bach and Handel. Both are very different worship expressions, but both are equally valid and essential. Elmer Towns summarizes this well when he states, "While there is a homogeneity in human nature and personality, cultural differences drive us to diversity... [and] the diversity of individuals accounts for the many expressions of worship. When all people worship God from their hearts, and in the comfort of their cultural expressions, God can touch and direct their lives."[3]

Sometimes, the argument arises that certain indigenous music is rooted in animistic and pagan cultures, and thus these musical styles are unsuitable for church use. European music, on the other hand, which is the basis of American hymnology, is rooted in the predominantly Christian culture of northern Europe. Thus, some hold the latter to be more suitable for the church.

However, the European notion of a choir originated within

the highly paganistic and mythological culture of the ancient Greeks. According to paintings found in the Tomb of Nakht in Thebes, stringed instruments were first employed by ancient Egyptians to worship Ra, the sun god. Yet, few people today would advocate eliminating choirs or stringed instruments from church participation because of their pagan genesis. In fact, Davidic music as described in the book of Psalms may have sounded much more like the syncopated and rhythmic music of Africa than European hymnology.

As stated earlier, cultural overhang most often affects our worship services. When planning a new church service, those of an older generation may require that elements of their musical or liturgical tastes be incorporated into the new celebration, even though it is targeted at a different generation. This often occurs because of an allegiance to a certain style of music that once accompanied a spiritual experience among the older generation. Thus, their suggestions are based upon a sincere longing to see these spiritual experiences reoccur in younger generations. Their motivation is laudable, but the direction is misguided. What they may not realize is that their cultural overhang is widening a generation gap, and making it difficult for the good news to cross over to the younger worshipers.

In addition, because certain forms of instrumentation, tempo, and melody are more well known, and thus more pleasant, we tend to ascribe familiar musical styles to the will of God. Cultural overhang becomes dangerous when we decide that, due to cultural familiarity or historic precedent, certain musical styles are more *divine* than others. What is true however, is that certain music styles are more *appropriate* than others, depending on which culture or generation is being reached. African American spirituals, with their rhythm-based cadence, introduced generations of slaves to spiritual liberation. While toiling under the unjust and atrocious system of slavery, they found hope expressed in music that combined the melody of their homelands with the power of the gospel and helped nurture in them a vibrant

Christianity. The South American church has appropriated the free-flowing rhythms of Latin America into songs of worship. In a similar manner, millions of Baby Boomers were introduced to Christian worship through the folk-rock styles of contemporary Christian music and praise choruses.

A Strategy for Indigenous Worship Expressions

In certain churches, musical tolerance and diversity is still controversial. In a few denominations, musical expression is forbidden altogether. But, in most venues, churches have experimented with a mixture of styles. However, to effectively eliminate cultural overhang, worship celebrations must be allowed to develop with an indigenous character. "Indigenous" means something that grows *naturally* in a region, country, or culture. The authors would suggest that this definition includes something that grows naturally in a *generational* culture, as well. Therefore, indigenous worship should have a structure, music, worship, teaching, length, and expression based on generational preferences. The word "indigenous" embraces the idea of culturally relevant, self-governing, and skilled worship expressions.

To encourage the rise of indigenous worship expressions, each worship expression should have a steering committee, team, or board comprised of the targeted generation. If cultural overhang is present among the leadership of a worship celebration, it will produce a culturally confusing and evangelistically impotent worship mixture. In addition, if there is no oversight committee to foster accountability and communication in a church, then a worship celebration can be out-of-sync and, at worst, divisive.

Therefore, as a church grows with different generations, it is best to organize parallel worship celebrations, each with their own format, leadership, and accountability structure. The organization of parallel worship services is one of the best methods for minimizing cultural friction.

In the Tri-Gen format, each parallel worship expression should have:

(1) **Its own worship style,** consisting of its own indigenous liturgy, musical forms, format, length, and teaching styles.

(2) **Its own leadership committee,** team, or board, which will oversee daily administration of the celebration.

(3) **A combined "executive committee,"** as described in chapter 6, to create a strong communication link between the church governing core (board or senior pastor) and the worship expression.

Therefore, each parallel worship celebration in a Tri-Gen church might be organized as shown in figure 8.1, which was first introduced in chapter 6.

How to Start An Indigenous Worship Celebration

How Many People Does It Take for Worship to Occur?

Usually, in a public setting, it requires approximately thirty-five adults for genuine worship to occur. In this environment, there are enough people to allow each person a moderate degree of privacy, while at the same time maintaining worship as a corporate event. Fewer than thirty-five people may make those new or unfamiliar with worship uncomfortable, feeling that everyone is noticing what they do, or do not do. A group of more than thirty-five people grants a degree of celebratory anonymity.

This is not to say that worship cannot break out in smaller groups, as it often does in the "cell"-sized group of three to twelve members. But, in the cell group, intimacy and emotional closeness allow such worship to break forth with small numbers. In some congregations, such cell groups are the location for most worship expressions. However, newcomers, or those unfamiliar with worship, usually find the intimacy and closeness of cell groups too intimidating at first.

Figure 8.1
Tri-Gen Church:

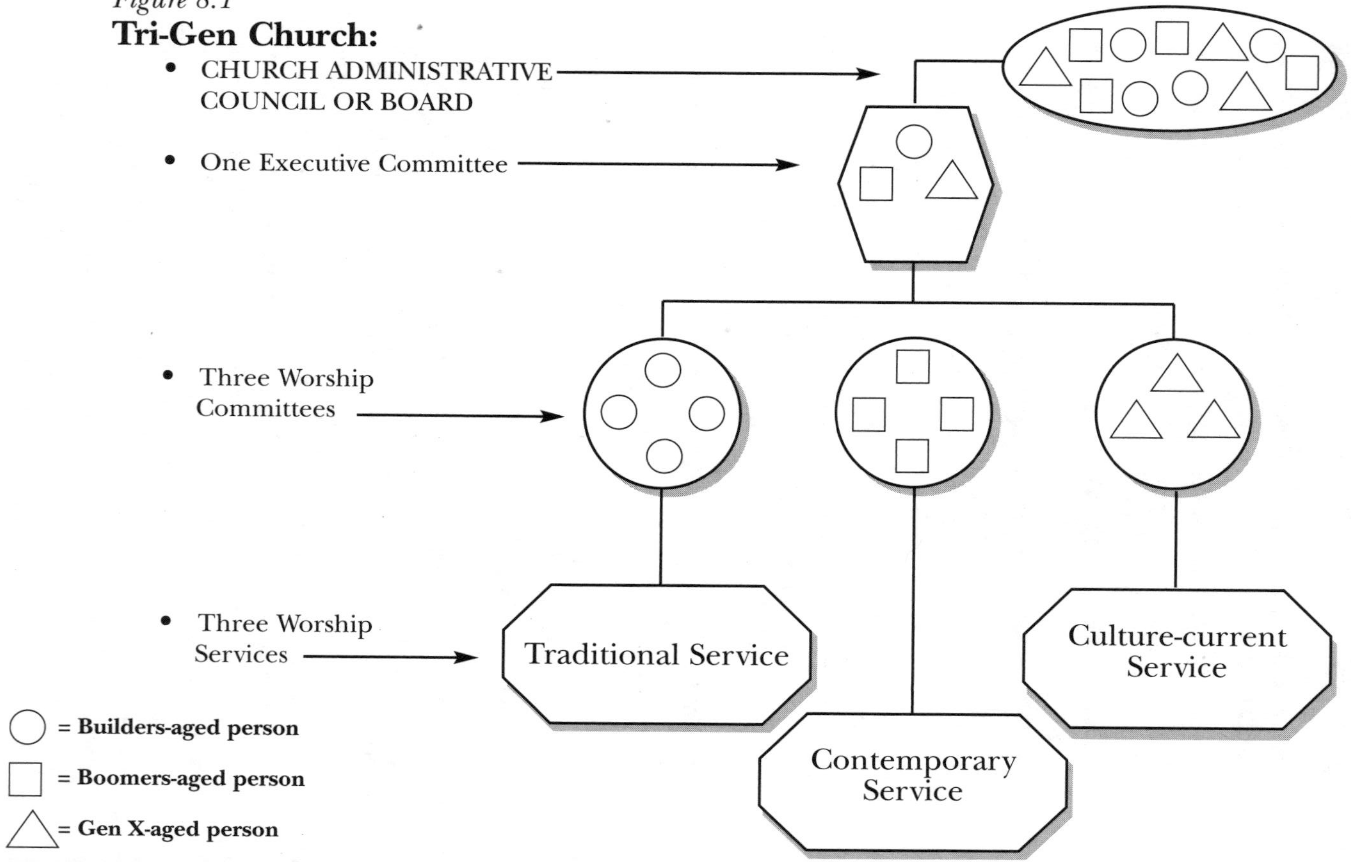

- CHURCH ADMINISTRATIVE COUNCIL OR BOARD

- One Executive Committee

- Three Worship Committees

- Three Worship Services

Traditional Service

Contemporary Service

Culture-current Service

○ = Builders-aged person

□ = Boomers-aged person

△ = Gen X-aged person

When strangers intermix with long-standing members, a minimum of thirty-five people gives a degree of privacy while ensuring the celebration reaches an event status in the minds of the participants. The worship experience as a communal event has a lot to commend it. Whether at the coronation of King Solomon in 1 Chronicles 29:20, or in the corporate worship of the seven Jewish festivals, coming together to worship God provided a sense of being part of something bigger.

But, Aren't "Blended Services" the Answer?

Services that blend together styles of two or more generations are widely practiced in America. Their purpose is to reach out to more than one generation at a time. These "blended" worship services often include several hymns for the Builder generation, along with a handful of choruses aimed at the Boomers and Generation X.

However, numerous interviews have led us to believe that, for most people, such blended formats feel erratic, unappetizing, and unfocused. Some interviewees noted that as soon as they began to enter into worship, their preferred musical style abruptly ended. The abridged and indistinct direction of a blended worship service seemed to thwart the very goal of the celebration—to lead persons into an encounter with a living God.

But, the blended service may be the only option for the church under eighty adult attendees, since thirty-five adults are usually required for worship to break out. For example, if a congregation of seventy-five attendees decides to initiate another celebration, the congregation could theoretically divide into two services of approximately thirty-five and forty people, so that these two services each would have the minimum of thirty-five persons needed. However, because worship style is a matter of personal taste and is often controversial, many people will prefer one service over the other, and others may refuse to attend altogether. The net result is that one of the services will probably not have the minimum thirty-five attendees. A usual outcome for a church of approximately seventy-five attendees is to have two services of fifty-five and twenty participants respectively. This, of course, dooms the smaller service. If your church is hovering between fifty and eighty in regular attendance, it will be prudent to wait until the congregation can muster nearly one hundred in adult attendance, before another service is inaugurated. Once this number has been attained, Step D of the Five Steps to Tri-generational Worship (discussed later in this chapter) will help you assemble the minimum number of attendees needed to inaugurate another worship celebration. Until then, the blended format may be a temporary and makeshift alternative.

Today, there are some churches that are large enough to host two services, but have embraced the blended strategy so firmly and for so long, that most congregants now prefer the blended format. "It gives me a variety in church," stated one elderly woman in Michigan. In Chicago, a middle-aged mother of teenagers observed, "I like the hymns and choruses; it's the best of both worlds." In most of these cases, the blended format has been in place for some time, and familiarity has bred appreciation.

The blended service may have thus become a stopgap strategy for smaller churches, and a permanent strategy for churches that have acquired a liking for such formats. But, if a church is seeking to reach out to unchurched people, the blended format will be culturally unconventional. Radio and television music marketers have purposely segmented the music market to drive up music sales. Marketers promote country music to one section of the populace, and classical music to another. One radio station will embrace a soft rock music format, and another the golden-oldie format. In addition, each generation is encouraged to embrace its own musical style as a statement of individuality and distinctiveness. The unconventional vocal style of Frank Sinatra was to the Builders what the unbridled merrymaking of the Beatles was to the Boomers. Today, Generation X embraces the unorthodox and atonal treatments of grunge and hip-hop music. Marketers know the power of encouraging generational distinctiveness, and, as a result, the free enterprise system has made America a world of segmented musical tastes. Although the blended format has become attractive to many church-goers, due to familiarity, to the unchurched, it often seems a half-hearted attempt to contemporize our message. And although the blended format cannot culturally relate enough to the unchurched, it will appeal to people who have an association with the church and are already familiar with the format. However, if the evangelism of the unchurched is a congregational goal, then moving away from blended formats and toward indigenous worship styles may not only be prudent, but necessary.

Different Generations Worship Differently

Different generations worship in different ways, due to familiarity and personal taste. However, before we look at some prototypical worship expressions, it is important to remember that, due to cross-generational surfers and even personal preference, not everyone will fall neatly into these categories. These categories are offered merely as general guidelines.

Builder Worship Styles

The generation born in 1945 and before was shaped by scarcity (due to the Great Depression) and sacrifice (due to World War II). This generation prefers worship that honors this heritage in its liturgy and traditions. Lutheran Builders value hymns that extol the sacrifice of Christ through the classical music of Johann Sebastian Bach and Felix Mendelssohn. Methodist Builders often enthusiastically embrace the simple refrains of Charles Wesley, although in his day, these songs were considered radically contemporary. In addition, Builders prefer liturgical uniformity which gives their increasingly insecure lives a degree of certainty. Thus, many Builders worship best with expressions that exude constancy, historical appreciation, and tradition.

Remember that in chapter 3, we saw how Builders often appreciate the effort that goes into a task even more than the outcome. Therefore, a less than perfect singer might be encouraged and praised for well-meaning effort, regardless of the outcome. Thus, Builders often worship in an atmosphere that embraces an appreciation for the effort expended over the outcome experienced.

The Builders' desire to worship God through their handiwork leads them to prefer traditional church buildings for their church services. Their nature as "builders" further leads them to prefer that the church be tidy, clean, and orderly; giving an appearance of self-respect and self-sufficiency.

Boomer Worship Styles

As was noted in earlier chapters, the Boomers want to improve everything. Since they have not been conditioned by the sacrifice and scarcity that molded their parents, they often can be perceived by their parents as squanderers of their birthright. In actuality, the Boomers are on a quest for enhancement and invention. They believe that new ways of doing things should replace old methods. Because of this, there arises a great deal of conflict with their Builder parents.

The Boomer wants the church to be up-to-date, professionally run, and of high quality. They want the pastor to address the important societal issues of the day, giving guidance from the Scriptures on controversial and divisive topics. They see traditions, liturgical standardization, and denominational history as monotonous and tedious. Their parents peered into the future and saw the ominous power of the atomic bomb, but the Boomer looks into the future and sees a world getting smaller and more advanced. While the Builder walks cautiously into the future, the Boomer charges ahead, haphazardly at times.

Therefore, Boomer celebrations are opportunities for experimentation. New ideas are not only allowed, but encouraged, since the scientific model allows for repeated experimentation and failure. This preference for experimentation greatly undermines the stability Builders seek. Thus, worship celebrations that seek to blend the two generations often create more controversy than celebration.

The Boomer does not share the Builder's attachment to a location or architectural style. The Boomer wants to make the church user-friendly by creating worship facilities that are accessible, well lit, cheery, and flexible. The Boomer celebration will find a multipurpose room, gymnasium, or warehouse more functional than a traditional sanctuary. The utilitarian character of their churches is an unspoken statement of their consumer-friendly approach to spreading the gospel.

The music of the Boomer celebration is extended, lively, and professional. The Boomer preference for quality means the Boomer celebration will place as high a value on outcome as intent. Mediocre music, which might be applauded in a Builder celebration, due to the effort expended, will not be tolerated in a Boomer format.

The music will be energetic in nature, as well, often eliciting hand clapping and rhythmic movement, something foreign to the Baroque spirit of the classical hymns. The worship music of Boomer churches tends to be consolidated into one or two extended passages. The Builder celebration might expect hymns to be peppered throughout the service, amid Scripture, responsive readings, and choral numbers. The Boomer celebration expects the music to be strung together, almost in an unbroken melodious stream that leads the worshiper into a spiritual encounter. It is not unusual for the worship portion of a Boomer celebration to last forty-five minutes or longer, with each song being delivered without a break, and building upon the last. The result for the Boomer worshiper is an uninterrupted encounter with God.

Generation X Worship Styles

In some ways, Generation X's worship style is a modern reworking of the styles of both the Builders and the Boomers. Generation X enjoys not only the hymns of their grandparents, but also the contemporary choruses of their parents. However, before you conclude that Gen-X will come to a worship service planned solely by Builders or Boomers, remember this—Gen-Xers want to put their own musical interpretation upon the music. Many popular choruses of Generation X are updated versions of the songs of their parents and grandparents. But, these updates carry a Generation X edginess that is often too unconventional for the Builders and Boomers. Whether it is a guitar driven version of "A Mighty Fortress Is Our God," or an up-tempo reggae interpretation of a slow Boomer chorus, Generation X seeks individuality.

Generation X seems to prefer an opportunity for interaction and intimacy in a worship celebration, as well. Allowing the attendees to break into small groups for prayer and sharing is popular. The Boomer prefers the anonymity of the large gathering, but the Gen-Xer seeks intimacy, even in the corporate venue. Generation X worship celebrations often allow extended periods of one-on-one interaction.

Finally, Generation X prefers worship that is fast-paced and multifaceted. Their church services are peppered with mixed media presentations, where a sermon might include snippets from a popular movie, a contemporary music video, and the evening news. Often, these mixed media formats are meant to draw a sharp contrast between the relativism of postmodern thought and the altruism of the Bible. With a quick succession of images, music, and scripture, Generation X worships in a milieu that is both rapid and relevant.

Five Steps to Tri-generational Worship

If a congregation has the number of attendees necessary to begin worshiping in a tri-generational format, how do you begin? Charles Arn, in *How to Start a New Service*, offers good research and proven ideas for adding another worship celebration. Steps A and C of the following were adapted in part from Arn's helpful treatise. Those wishing further insights on these steps should consult his helpful volume.[4]

Step A: Whom Are You Targeting?

The first step in starting a new service is to use the tools discussed in chapter 6 to identify the generation at which this new celebration is aimed.

However, there is a caveat here. If you are targeting a generation other than the dominant generation in your current celebration, do not try to target a different ethnicity as well. If you change too many variables, the chance of success is greatly reduced. In other words, if yours is a predominantly Hispanic and Builder congregation, start a celebration that reaches Boomer or Generation X Hispanics. Do not attempt to start a celebration aimed at Anglo Boomers, for in doing so, you have changed too many variables, both age and ethnicity. In the same manner, a predominantly white Boomer congregation should either start a new service to reach Boomers of another ethnicity (Boomer Koreans for example[5]) or start a new service to reach Generation Xers of their own (Anglo) culture. Starting a new service that changes both ethnicity and age in the target audience contains too many variables to be successful.

Step B: When Will You Offer This Service?

The second step is to ask yourself, "When will we offer an additional celebration?" Our consultative work has led us to believe there are certain times that are more beneficial than others. In figures 8.2, 8.3, and 8.4 we have listed the best times for such celebrations, according to our research. However, these are generalizations sampled across a broad spectrum of churches. The unique contextual factors of your community may mean the order of popularity in your community may differ. If you feel this is the case, you can determine the most popular service times for your community by adding appropriate questions to the need assessment survey discussed in chapter 7.

173

Figure 8.2

**The Most Popular Worship Times for Builders
in Order of Popularity**

Sunday Morning

Wednesday Evening This ranks a very distant second behind
Sunday morning in all three generations.
Sunday morning is usually preferred 4 to 1
over any other time during the week. Thus,
if at all possible, Sunday morning should be
utilized.

Sunday Evening

**Any Weekday Evening,
except Friday**

Friday Evening

Saturday Evening This is the least popular time for Builders.

Figure 8.3

**The Most Popular Worship Times for Boomers
in Order of Popularity**

Sunday Morning

Saturday Evening Among Boomers, Saturday evening ranks
second, but like Wednesday evening with
the Builders, it ranks a very distant second
behind Sunday morning. Again, use
Sunday morning if at all possible.

Wednesday Evening

**Any Weekday Evening,
except Friday**

Sunday Evening

Friday Evening Friday evening is the least popular time for
Boomers.

Figure 8.4

**The Most Popular Worship Times for Generation X
in Order of Popularity**

Sunday Morning

Saturday Evening   As with Boomers, Saturday evening ranks a distant second behind Sunday morning.

Friday Evening   This ranks higher for Generation X than for other generations, in part because many Gen-Xers are delaying marriage. Friday night, therefore, becomes a night for socializing, such as at church celebrations. As they mature and marry, weeknights will replace Friday at this spot on this list.

Wednesday Evening

Any Weekday Evening, except Friday

But see Whatever Change Reaction p. 63

Sunday Evening   This ranks lowest in popularity because many Gen-Xers now work on Saturdays, so Sunday is their only day to address household tasks and responsibilities. Going to church on an evening before the start of the work week often prevents them from completing tasks such as grocery shopping, laundry, cleaning, and preparation for the work week.

Since Sunday morning appears to be the most advantageous time for all three generations, the next question is "What time on Sunday is best?" We have ranked the Sunday morning scheduling options in order of desirability in figure 8.5. Again, these are generalizations, gleaned from a broad spectrum of churches. Use the following scheduling options as guidelines, not rigid rules.

Figure 8.5

Ranked Options for Multiple Worship Services
on Sunday Morning

1. The best time to hold another service is before or after the existing church service(s) and the Sunday school hour. Sometimes congregations will try to conduct concurrent worship services, but this places significant demands upon volunteers, making it a difficult route for both the small church and the smaller medium-sized church. However, in the larger medium-sized church, as well as in the large congregation where multiple staff persons and ample parking are available, this can be a viable option. However, for most churches the best time will be before or after the existing service and Sunday school, as long as the new service fits in a window between 8 A.M. to noon.

2. Some congregations will discover their second best option is to hold the new service during the existing Sunday school hour. When Sunday school is before or after the existing service, this means the sanctuary may be available. Of course, this strategy means that attendees at the new service will not be able to attend Sunday school. Because the Sunday school often provides the needed small or "cell" group interaction of many churches, it is recommended if this route be taken that another Sunday school hour eventually be inaugurated.

3. Sometimes facility resources will be so stretched that it may be necessary to hold the new service at a different location than the church facility. At other times this may be a strategic decision to allow the new celebration to free itself from an overly religious environment. Regardless of the reason, this is called the "campus" approach to the tri- generational church. It can be attractive to unchurched people, but it can also work against unity and identity. Therefore, starting a new service at another venue must be approached cautiously and circumspectly to ensure it does not impair identity and unity.

Step C: What Will Your New Service Look Like?

This depends on the generation that you target with your new service. Regardless of the generation approached, Charles Arn reminds us that the entire service—not just the sermon—must be the message carrier. Arn states, "*The sermon is not the message; the service is the message.* . . . The message is conveyed via the *entire* service" (italics his).[6] What Arn means is that a twenty-five-minute sermon must not be the only message carrier. The worship, the liturgy, the welcome of visitors, drama, special music, and so forth, all must be part of a generational approach that holds forth the service's central message.

In addition, the authors would add that a spiritual encounter is also an integral part of the worship service. The message conveyed at a worship service should lead congregants to an encounter with the God who can meet the needs the message describes. It is only when humans come into contact with their Creator that a spiritual encounter occurs that makes the message achievable. Thus, the goal of a holistic church service should be to inculcate a consistent, practical, and applicable message that begs a spiritual encounter. The result of this should be that the congregant is given the hope and assurance that he or she is not alone or adrift.

The exact composition of a new church service requires prayer and reflection. Many churches have found it helpful to designate a worship committee or planning team comprised of the age group they seek to attract. Then, it is beneficial to have this planning group spend an extended period of time together in prayer and planning. It is here that the exact composition of the new service will emerge. Usually, this planning stage will begin a minimum of three months before the new service is inaugurated.

Step D: Why Do Crowds Attract Crowds?

One of the most neglected tasks is getting enough people to attend at the onset of a new service. As noted earlier in this chapter, it often requires attendance of thirty-five or more people to experience a degree of corporate worship. However, Charles Arn's research indicates that the average new service can expect up to a 25 percent decline in the first months.[7] Success of the new service often depends upon a congregation not declining below the thirty-five attendance number, even after a potential 25 percent decline is factored in. Thus, the minimum number for a new celebration should be approximately forty-seven individuals. In addition, this number can be higher if the room is large. Therefore, it is wise to assess how many people above a minimum of thirty-five you can expect. Then adjust the room size with dividers or change the venue. Ideally, the facility should feel at least 60 percent full when the service is inaugurated with a minimum of forty-seven individuals.

The best way to attain your minimum number of attendees is to solicit volunteers to launch the new worship service. These should be attending members who understand and appreciate the cultural differences of each generation. It should be explained to them that they are going to be experiencing a new form of worship, and that though they may feel culturally uncomfortable, they must tenaciously support the new endeavor. Churches have succeeded by asking forty-five or more members to commit a minimum of one year to attending this new service. This method is similar to an indigenous foreign mission strategy, where a missionary voluntarily undergoes cultural adaptation to reach new people. In our tri-generational adaptation, at the end of one year, each person will be expected to have replaced themselves with one attendee from the target generation.

Finally, the news of your new celebration must be carried by two avenues—personal invitations and public announcement. Many congregations make the mistake of relying heavily upon public announcements rather than personal invitations. Personal invitations are the most potent form of evangelism, with some studies showing that 80 percent or more of a congregation's growth will take place through personal invitations of friends, acquaintances, relatives, and neighbors.[8]

Step E: Prayer

Because bringing people to Christ is a work of the Holy Spirit, ongoing prayer for the unchurched becomes our highest priority. Before any service is inaugurated, it is important that extended, heartfelt, and ardent prayer be offered for its format, participants, and potential attendees. So critical is prayer to the success of every area of the tri-generational model, that we have allocated the entirety of chapter 10 to it.

Keeping the Doors Open to the Unchurched

Fifteen Minutes That Can Change the World

Once unchurched people attend your new celebration, you must offer them a clearly defined route into the life of the congregation. Most people decide if they like a congregation within the first fifteen minutes. Thus, long before the pastor has a chance to preach, or the soloist has a chance to sing his or her most polished tune, the visitors have usually made up their mind about returning.

Churches that understand this social phenomena, and are prepared for it, can reap a significant harvest in the first fifteen minutes. In fact, these fifteen minutes can be the interval that changes your community. To best utilize the beginning fifteen minutes, two key ideas must be employed.

(1) Publicly greet visitors from the podium within the first fifteen minutes. Let them know you are here to help them. Do not talk about all the good things they can do for *you* and *your* church. Do not

talk about volunteer opportunities or the church's "needs." Rather, tell them about your vision to help *them*. Let them know what to expect in the upcoming minutes. Tell them they may stay seated if they are so inclined, and because they are guests, they are not expected to give when the offering is received. One church requested that everyone put the offering envelopes found in the bulletin into the offering plate as it passed so the envelopes could be "recycled." This allowed visitors not to feel singled out because they had not prepared a financial gift. In addition, do nothing publicly that makes your guests stand out, such as forcing them to rise or giving them a ribbon with "visitor" printed on it. Allow your visitors to retain a measure of public anonymity.

(2)   However, it is important that you allow the newcomers to meet several regular attendees in the first fifteen minutes. When people attend a church, they are first and foremost asking the social question, "Are there people like me here?" People feel more comfortable receiving the good news from people like themselves. Therefore, a short time where people can mingle and introduce themselves to one another is essential. People today are not often skilled in making meaningful conversation during these opportunities. Therefore, the helpful memory device, F.O.R.M. can deepen conversations.

F = Family. First, get to know something about their family. How old are their children, and which school do they attend? If children are not present, inquire about a family name and you may discover mutual friends or interests.

O = Occupation. Whatever a person does for forty or more hours a week is going to be of at least passing interest. Ask about their vocation, what they like about their work (keep it positive), and how long they have been involved in this occupation (but not how long they have worked for a certain employer).

R = Recreation. Ask your guests what they do for recreation and about their hobbies. Do they ski, bike, swim, golf, or raise championship dogs? Do they enjoy knitting, model building, gardening, or travel?

M = Ministry they need. Though the F, O, and R may be easily covered in a few minutes at the beginning of a church service, specific ministry they may need will take time to discover. Therefore, do not try to reach this step until you have met them on several occasions. However, it is important to remember that getting to know someone is not fully developed until we have learned about the needs that have brought them to Christ and His church.

Newcomer Follow-up

It is crucial to follow up your newcomers. Elmer Towns's experience has led him to posit a "law of seven contacts."[9] Towns is convinced that visitors make a meaningful decision to return and become regular attendees only after they have been contacted by the church seven times. Seeing the church's ad in a newspaper or yellow pages can suffice for a contact, as can a letter from the pastor or lay leader. Towns discovered that telephone calls, tactfully placed by members of the congregation on Sunday afternoon and the following Saturday morning, can also have great effect. The law of seven contacts reminds us that follow through is as important as personal invitations and public announcements. Diplomatically and fully welcoming the newcomer into your fellowship lets one know you are interested in his or her felt needs.

A newcomer's class is another very important step in the assimilation process. Some studies have shown that unless a newcomer becomes a part of a small group within two weeks of deciding to join a church, the person will eventually become a dropout.[10]

A class designed to answer the newcomer's inaugural questions is an excellent way to introduce your guests to the small group life of the church. Remember, small group theory suggests that a cell (small) group is a group of three to twelve people characterized by intimacy and interpersonal involvement. For some congregations, these will be weeknight "kinship" or "home" groups. For many other churches, cell groups are primarily the Sunday school classes.

Regardless of which type of cell groups you possess, the newcomer class should take place at the same time as the majority of your other cell groups. While your guest is attending a newcomer class, he or she is becoming accustomed to gathering at the designated cell group time. For example, if a newcomer class is held on Sunday morning during the Sunday school hour, the attendees will be accustomed to being at church at this hour. In addition, child care will be available. Once the newcomer class has run its course, the attendees can join another cell group at that hour or form their own. Either way, meeting at a time concurrent to your other cell groups allows a newcomer class to evolve into something permanent.

The question arises as to whether the newcomer class should be limited to one generation or be transgenerational in composition. This will depend on two factors, your church size and the age of the guests that are visiting your church. First, if a church is in the medium (201–400) to large (401+) size range, it can and should establish newcomer cell groups based on generational preferences. Small groups that have a generational ambience will be more attractive and more cohesive. It is not necessarily essential to announce publicly that these are generation-specific groups, any more than it is with any other cell group. Usually the generational character of the group will be evident in the leadership involved, the topics discussed, and the way the groups are promoted.

Second, the age of the visitors that God is sending to your church will be a determining factor. This is especially true in a small church where person power is limited. In smaller venues (200 or less attendees), a newcomer class may have to be transgenerational, due to a limited number of volunteers available, as well as to meet the needs of several generations at one time. However, if God is primarily sending you newcomers from one age group, then the character of the class may need to be leaning toward them. To determine the age of your visitors it is often helpful to have guests register on a small card that includes a box to check off their birth year (such as depicted in figure 6.5). Subsequently you can design a newcomer class that is led by, and geared to, a specific generation.

People also wonder what curriculum should be used in such classes. First, resist the temptation to use membership curriculum. Membership is a deeper step into accountability and the life of a congregation. It should be employed, but not at the outset. Think of membership as marriage, and a newcomer class as dating. The newcomer class's purpose is to acquaint potential members with the mission, vision, and personality of your church.

Consequently, a newcomer class should be designed to answer the most pressing questions the visitor has about the church. Our research has uncovered five questions that consistently rank among the top questions all three generations are asking about a host congregation. However, they vary in popularity among each generation. Figure 8.6 compares the rankings of "The Top Five Questions" newcomers are asking.

Figure 8.6

THE TOP FIVE QUESTIONS
NEWCOMERS ASK ABOUT A CHURCH

Ranking	Generation X	Boomer	Builder
1.	Range of Ministries Available	Range of Ministries Available	Beliefs of the Congregation
2.	Church Government	Church Finances	Denominational History
3.	Church Finances	Church Government	Range of Ministries Available
4.	Denominational History	Beliefs of the Congregation	Church Government
5.	Beliefs of the Congregation	Denominational History	Church Finances

Now, let us define what is meant by each question.

Range of Ministries Available

Most of the time, people want to first know what ministries a church offers. Among Boomers and Generation X, this is the number one question newcomers ask, and it ranks number three for the Builders. Promptly addressing this question is a good way to let your newcomers know about the multifaceted life of your congregation. Many churches respond to this by offering a small brochure, but unfortunately they do not go further and address the other questions newcomers are asking.

Church Finances

Two decades ago, this question would not have made our list. However, in today's cynical world, questions about a church's solvency and financial stability are commonplace. Even a simple piechart that shows that an inordinate amount of money is not spent on administration and salaries can be very helpful. Boomers in particular, who are accustomed to scrutinizing stock and investment prospecti, will not allow the church to dismiss financial disclosures.

Church Government

Another question that years ago would not have made our list is the question of how a church is organized and governed. The popularity of this question can be traced to an emerging cynical nature among younger generations. Generation X especially wants to know if there is accountability for the leadership as well as clear lines of communication. As we saw in chapter 3, Generation X's skeptical nature arises in part due to the splits and closures they witnessed in their parents' congregations. In addition, this question is important for Boomers, because of their desire to clearly understand the route to church involvement.

Beliefs of the Congregation

What a church believes regarding issues of faith is important to the newcomer. Often, the designation Baptist, Methodist, or Presbyterian will tell newcomers very little about the beliefs of the individual church. Thus, we are using the term "beliefs of the congregation" to mean not only exploring the creedal statement of faith, but also discussing issues embraced by the local congregation.

Although Builders are usually familiar with denominational labels, they know better than most that churches of the same denomination can vary widely in belief. Thus, Builders will want to know your position on the role of women in the church, your theological persuasion (conservative, moderate, or liberal), and your sacramental practices. Boomers and Generation X, on the other hand, will

185

want to know your stance on more culture-current and controversial issues such as abortion, homosexuality, and divorce.

Regardless of the generation, the best place to address these issues is at the onset, so that differences can lead to either bonding or departure.

Denominational History

Younger newcomers will usually have only a fuzzy idea about denominational histories and distinctiveness. However, a brief denominational history can put the past in perspective, drawing out lessons and appreciation. Builders also enjoy revisiting a renowned denominational heritage, and those not from your affiliation will often find parallels with their own historical faith community. In fact, revisiting or discovering the denominational history helps Builders see the church in its historical context. For the Builder, this introduces a feeling of historical stability and constancy into their increasingly precarious lives.

Churches that quickly and clearly address these "top five" questions will be embracing a proactive stance toward guests of all generations. And inaugurating a newcomer class is not much more difficult than starting a new Sunday school class or other cell group. Many times, a newcomer class is organized around a five-week cycle, with one week being given to cover each of the five questions listed in figure 8.6. One person can "host" the newcomer class and invite special guests from various departments to each address one of the five topics, one per week. A person from the Finance Committee might address finances one week, while a person from the Administrative Council could address church government another. With this type of format, the newcomer class does not yield to boredom, but ushers in a stream of church leaders who meet and teach the newcomers about your church.

Unity Building Exercises: Unity Services

In a tri-generational church, retaining unity in the face of increasing diversity can become a challenge. Of the seven steps, Step 1 covered in chapter 5 gives helpful ways to explain how unity can thrive in diversity. However, one of the most practical methods for encouraging unity is the periodic "unity celebration."

A unity celebration is a once-a-quarter or twice-a-year combined worship event. At this celebration, the Builder worship celebration, the Boomer celebration, as well as the Generation X celebration forgo their individual worship services to cooperatively sponsor a grand combined service. This combined service allows the church members to see the true size of a tri-generational congregation. Often it will be so large that it will require the use of another facility, such as a school gymnasium or a local arena. The magnitude of this gathering will not only help foster the overall identity of the congregation, but it will also demonstrate to the community the true size of the congregation.

The unity service format is simple—showcase the best that each generation has to offer. The Builder choir should bring its best musical numbers, while the Boomer praise band should offer its most polished and uplifting choruses. Drama and/or mixed-media presentations by Generation X can tell how the good news is being spread among a postmodern culture. Guests will find this an exciting and pan-generational introduction to the whole congregation.

A unity event should be a celebration of one Lord among different generations. Short testimonies are often helpful, allowing members of different generations to witness the move of the Holy Spirit among different ages and through different methodologies. If such suggestions are followed, the end result of a unity celebration can be a heightened identity, both internally and externally.

Chapter Nine

STEP 5: Befriending and Inviting

Find the Bridges and Use Them

What Are the Bridges of God?

"It happened almost like you described it would," responded this forty–something mother of two. "It was easier than you made it out to be, but took longer than you said," added her husband. As we sat in the foyer of an imposing seventy-three-year-old church, these church members recounted their recent success in introducing a young couple to their church. This Boomer couple had been members of First Church for almost a decade, but aside from some early successes, they had brought no one to the church in almost eight-and-a-half years. After a recent clinic on how the "bridges of God" can help reach new generations, they had decided to reach out to a young Generation X couple that had recently moved next door.

"First, I offered him any help or tools he might need...he didn't borrow anything, but we got to know each other," the husband explained. "They were from downstate, and she didn't have a gynecologist; I helped her find one in our area," added his wife. "The capper was when we invited them to a (Detroit) Pistons game," continued the husband. "We had some time to talk and get to know each other. It was simple to tell them about our church." A few minutes later the wife interjected, "It took a lot of invitations, but after they visited the church they really liked it....They've got some of their friends coming now and have their own (Sunday school) class." "How long did this process take?" I inquired. "Eight years for us; seven months for them," she responded.

Their church was now enjoying an influx of Gen-Xers who were acquaintances of the couple they had befriended. Soon, this church began to grow among a younger generation that had formerly been absent, and all because of an important, but often overlooked, principle called the "bridges of God."

The term "bridges of God" was coined by Donald A. McGavran in a book by the same title in 1955.[1] Researching foreign missionary strategies, McGavran discovered that faith spreads most naturally across social networks of friends, associates, relatives, and neighbors. He called these social networks over which the good news easily travels the "bridges of God." Later, in his extensive study on church growth, *Understanding Church Growth*, McGavran stated, "Again and again I observed that though Christians are surrounded by fellow citizens, the Christian faith flows best from relative to relative or close friend to close friend. This was true whatever the nationality or language. It was as true in the heartland of America as in Uganda or the High Andes."[2]

To illustrate this, McGavran suggested that society be thought of as a town built on two sides of a river, with the church on one side and unchurched people on the other. Bridges exist between the two sides, over which "ideas, foodstuffs, processions, and convictions flow to and fro across the bridges."[3] It was across these social bridges that the good news could most readily travel to unchurched family and friends. The key is to identify to whom these social bridges exist and then with prayer and presentation send the good news across. George Hunter, one of the sharpest theological minds on this subject, put it in a slightly more technical manner: "Non-Christians are much more receptive to credible

Christian kinsmen or friends than to strangers, or even known members of other subcultures."[4]

Research has supported the existence and potency of these bridges. Win Arn polled 4,000 adult converts and found that 70 to 80 percent of the people who become church attendees did so because of a personal invitation delivered by a friend or relative. Arn's research, as demonstrated in figure 9.1, indicates that invitations across social networks are the principle routes of entry into our churches.

Figure 9.1

Reasons People Join a Church[5]

Percentage	Reasons
6–8	Just walked in
2–3	Came through the church's program
8–12	The pastor attracted them
3–4	Came out of a special need
1–2	Were visited by church members
3–4	Came through a Sunday school class
0.5	Came because of a city-wide evangelistic campaign
70–80	**Invited by friends or relatives**

Why Are the Bridges of God
Frequently Neglected?

The bridges of God are often overlooked because once a person has been a Christian for some time, one's contact with nonchurched people is diminished. Christians develop with each other a natural intimacy and attachment that soon bonds them together, but unfortunately insulates them from unchurched people.

In addition, generational clannishness increases the tendency for intimacy and attachment to develop. An unfortunate result is that generational bonding within the church further disengages Christians from unchurched people, even those of their own generation. Therefore, in all churches, but especially those embracing the tri-generational format, it becomes imperative that, as we celebrate generational distinctiveness, we do not lose sight of the bridges of God that link us to the unchurched people of our generation.

Let us use McGavran's analogy of a town to illustrate the above points. Society is like a town built on two sides of a river, where one side is the church and the other is non-churchgoing people, or those we have described in this book as unchurched people. Although the sides are connected by bridges, some people live nearer the bridges. These usually are people who have recently crossed the bridges, and subsequently they have more contact with unchurched people. After a person has been a church member for a number of years, he or she unconsciously moves farther from the bridges, as social networks start to pull one toward other Christians rather than to unchurched people. Among second and third generation Christians, this problem is even more pronounced.

McGavran paints a dismal picture of what happens when our churches lose sight of the bridges of God. McGavran draws an example from the church in India.

In India the first generation of Christians was very conscious of its non-Christian relatives. But second and third generation Christians, most of whom have not come to Christ by conversion from non-Christian religions, but by biological church growth, know few if any non-Christian relatives. They do not attend their weddings or funerals. Each group of relatives has shut the other out of its life. The bridges long neglected have fallen into disrepair. Some have been swept away by floods. Such churches, having no bridges, have become ethnic enclaves, or, in plain words, ghettos. Neglect of bridges leads to that dismal outcome.[6]

When the bridges of God have been abandoned what can be done? A church must rediscover and refurbish the bridges. The bridges are not destroyed, only derelict, and with some effort, they can be refitted and recrossed.

How to Rebuild Your Bridges of God: Befriending

Rediscovering the bridges of God may require a bit of effort at the onset. Time and acculturation may have distanced you spiritually from your friends, relatives, acquaintances and neighbors. New habits and habitats may have removed you from the midst of unchurched people of your generation. Sadly, unintended yet sanctimonious attitudes may have raised barriers between the unchurched and the Christian community.

However, crossing the bridges is not only necessary, but mandated by biblical example. Barnabas utilized the bridges of God to reach his fellow countrymen on Cyprus during his first and second missionary journeys (Acts 13:1-12; 15:39*b*). Paul visited Galatian cities near his ancestral home in Tarsus on all three missionary journeys (Acts 13:1–14:20, 15:36–20:38). When Andrew, a disciple of John the Baptist, heard Jesus speak, "the first thing [Andrew] did was to find his brother Simon and tell him, 'We have found the Messiah' (that is, the Christ). And he brought him to Jesus" (John 1:41-42).

Recovering your bridges of God can be accomplished in four steps:

(1) **Look around and see the many bridges that still exist or can be developed between yourself and unchurched people.** Here, it is helpful to make a list of unchurched people you can reach toward. Many of these will be people from your generation. But some will be from other generations as well. Do not limit yourself to recovering only those bridges that link you to people of your own generation. A strong bridge to a relative or neighbor from another generation may be as potent as a bridge to a friend or acquaintance from the same generation. Keep an open mind and you will discover there are many more bridges than you realized.

(2) **Enough time must be allocated to redevelop these bridges.** Bridges disintegrate slowly over time, and it may take a proportional amount of time to refit them.

(3) **Bridges can be developed through proximity, generational inclination, and shared interest.** Inviting an unchurched person to a sporting or social event allows for a casual time of sharing and getting acquainted. Cookouts, camping trips, picnics, excursions, sightseeing trips, hobbies, car pooling, community projects, and acts of kindness are only a few ways to get to know others who do not yet attend church.

(4) **To befriend unchurched people is the goal of this process.** Churches must be prepared to nonjudgmentally befriend people who are not church

attendees and, in many cases, are not Christian. This will require long hours of bridge building mingled with a great deal of tolerance. Avoiding controversial topics and not judging lifestyles will be key to the befriending process. Befriending people of the same generation will also help circumnavigate this hazard, but not completely eradicate it. To truly befriend others you must genuinely love and accept others, while allowing the Holy Spirit to work upon them in His time. Though you are the vessel, it is the wind of the Spirit that provides the direction, impetus, and conviction.

Who Are the Receptive People?

People with Change in Their Lives

The bridges of God can be crossed the easiest when the person who is the object of our befriending strategy is looking for friendship, stability, and/or guidance. These people are already seeking bridges to wholeness, friendship, and spirituality. Because of this desire, they will even help you construct a bridge to reach them. Examples of people who are looking for bridges of support and assistance include (but are not limited to):

People who are experiencing a new phase in their lives

Marriage	Going off to school	Empty-nest syndrome
Divorce	Returning from	(last child leaving
Separation	school	home)
A new job	A new house	Middle-age transition
Loss of a job	First child leaving	Retirement
A new child	home	Death of a loved one

People who have lost faith (in anything)

George Hunter offers some excellent insights on America's infatuation with quasi-religious devotion. Hunter notes that America is "characterized by religious anarchy," and that the church that is reaching out should "constantly be on the lookout for people 'between idols.'"[7]

People who are experiencing problems or difficulties in their lives

Financial problems	Extended family	Health problems
Marital problems	problems	Social and relational
Child-rearing	Employment	problems
problems	problems	

F.R.A.N.s

Elmer Towns has given us an easy to remember acronym for people to whom bridges may be built, calling them "F.R.A.Ns."[8] This mnemonic device helps us recall that the most receptive people will be our "Friends, Relatives, Associates, and Neighbors." These are people with whom bridges of God exist or potentially exist, even though presently they may be in dire need of repair or completion. Friends and neighbors will often, but not exclusively, be of the same generation as yourself.

In a similar manner, relatives and associates will many times be of another generation. Therefore, be careful not to limit yourself strictly to befriending and inviting F.R.A.Ns of the same generation.

Figures 9.2, 9.3, 9.4, and 9.5 give examples of the type of persons that will fit into each of these categories. As you look at the following figures, you may notice that there are more people in each category than you formerly realized.

Figure 9.2

	F.R.A.Ns	
	Friends	
	A. People with whom you enjoy hobbies and sports	
1. Golfing	2. Fishing	3. Singing
4. Skiing	5. Tennis	6. Model building
7. Basketball	8. Football	9. Bowling
10. Camping	11. Biking	12. Skating
13. Photography	14. Painting	15. Volleyball
16. Drama	17. Handicrafts	18. Cooking
19. Woodworking	20. Sewing	21. Music
22. Metalworking	23. Needlepoint	24. Collecting
25. Bridge	26. Chess	27. Swimming

B. People with whom you regularly socialize by

1. Dining out	2. Attending sporting events and concerts	3. Participating in community organizations
4. Attending artistic events	5. Shopping and traveling	6. Participating in charitable activities
7. Attending school functions	8. Participating in volunteer activities	9. Sharing carpools, trains, buses, and subways

Figure 9.3

F.R.A.Ns Relatives		
1. Brothers	2. Sisters	3. Parents
4. Children	5. Grandchildren	6. Grandparents
7. Aunts	8. Uncles	9. Cousins
10. Godparents	11. Godchildren	12. In-laws
13. Stepparents	14. Stepchildren	15. Extended relations
16. Foster parents	17. Foster children	18. Half siblings

Figure 9.4

F.R.A.Ns Associates A. People who help or serve you		
1. Dentist	2. Doctor	3. Mechanic
4. Banker	5. Grocer	6. Waiter/Waitress
7. Clerk	8. Counter person	9. Gas attendant
10. Plumber	11. Baker	12. Handyman
13. School teacher	14. Counselor	15. Community volunteer
16. Business owner	17. Politician	18. Public utilities person
19. Newspaper carrier	20. Postman	21. Police or fire department persons

B. People who belong to the same group as you		
1. Social clubs	2. Professional associations	3. Community organizations
4. Service clubs	5. Luncheon or dinner clubs	6. Special interest clubs and gatherings
7. Parent-teacher associations	8. Fraternal associations	9. Educational associations
C. People you work with		
1. People you supervise	2. Students you teach	3. Secretaries
4. Clerical staff	5. Supervisors	6. Clients
7. New staff	8. Former staff	9. Colleagues
10. People you serve or assist	11. People who assist you	12. People who work in close proximity
13. People you see while traveling to work	14. People with whom you eat lunch	15. People with whom you travel

Figure 9.5

F.R.A.Ns Neighbors		
1. Immediate neighbors	2. New neighbors	3. Elderly neighbors
4. Young neighbors	5. Neighbors in transition	6. Neighbors you meet socially
7. Neighbors with whom you borrow or share items	8. Neighbors with common interests	9. Neighbors who need their walk shoveled, grass mowed, or leaves raked
10. Neighbors with families like yours	11. Neighbors with small children	12. Neighbors with teenagers

The Law of Multiple Invitations

In chapter 8, we noted that Elmer Towns has postulated a social law he calls the "law of seven contacts." According to Towns, "A person usually makes a meaningful decision for Christ after the church has contacted him seven times."[10] The present authors have witnessed a corollary to this law which we call the "law of multiple invitations."

The same social laws that underpin the "law of seven contacts" are also behind the "law of multiple invitations." Our experience has led us to believe that people must be invited multiple times before their commitments and calendars allow them to accept the invitation.[11] Regrettably, many Christians give up before multiple invitations are given. Not wanting to socially suffocate a person, many people discontinue their invitations after a few rejections. Often the rejection is based upon time and convenience, rather than a distaste for the invitation.

Why Are Multiple Invitations Necessary?

The hectic lifestyle of most people today has made time the commodity of the new millennium. In other words, people so highly value their time that they will only make a decision to add something new to their schedule after they have assessed it extensively and are sure it is worth the time required. Because of the magnitude of the decision, most people cannot make such judgments rapidly or quickly. People need added information and more time to assess if the new opportunity meshes well with their life goals and current activities. Many times an inviter gives up after a few invitations, when in actuality the person invited may just need more information and more assessment. Subsequently, it is imperative that an inviter is tenacious, tactful, and not easily discouraged.

Thus, an inviter must be prepared to practice patience, while tactfully delivering more information. Armed with tenacity and diplomacy, an inviter will find that results usually occur according to the law of multiple invitations.

How Many Invitations Are Needed?

The number of invitations necessary to ensure a positive response will vary greatly due to circumstances surrounding the invitation and the appeal (or lack thereof) of the activity. Therefore, the authors have resisted the idea of assigning a hard and fast number to the amount of invitations needed, preferring to stress the significance of the multiplicity of the invitations, rather than a precise figure. However, many have requested a general idea of the numbers involved. Therefore, with some hesitancy, we explain that experience has led us to believe that between five and seven invitations are common. This average seems to hold up across generations, though for different reasons. Having said this, we caution the reader not to rely on any average, but rather to employ the number of multiple invitations necessary to ensure that scheduling and/or lack of assessment is not the source of an invitation's rejection.

How Does a Church Practice Multiple Invitations?

How can this law of multiple invitations be adopted into the life of the church? A three-sided approach is best.

(1) **Plan visitor events early, allowing plenty of time for the inviter to tender multiple invitations.** Events should be planned at least seven weeks in advance, and church members who are planning to bring friends should be given at least five weeks for invitations. In such a scenario, an inviter could possibly tender one invitation a week to a receptive person.

(2) **Second, invitations should not be mundane, covering the same ground again and again.** Instead, the church should highlight the numerous virtues of the upcoming event. To stimulate this, the

church may wish to announce each week another merit of the upcoming event. This approach not only gives congregants multifaceted information, but it also makes their invitations varied and befitting.

(3) **Third, the need for multiple invitations must be mentioned frequently from the pulpit and elsewhere.** The purpose here is to remind the church of the law of multiple invitations.

We must rediscover and refit the bridges of God, then be prepared to cross them with invitations that are as tenacious as they are tactful. When bridges are crossed, by men and women resolutely committed to befriend those on the other side, the church will rise to William Carey's memorable challenge, "Attempt great things for God and expect great things from God."

Chapter Ten

STEP 6: Evaluate Your Success

No Substitute for Evaluation

Thwarting the Choke Law

It was another of those phrases that resonated loudly with our experience. In *10 Steps to Church Growth*, Donald McGavran and Win Arn had told of a Tanzanian missionary who warned that strategies are doomed to fail, if they do not take into account the "choke law." This law is what happens when a church grows and existing members start "to absorb the entire time, attention, and budget of both laymen and pastors."[1] A subsequent maintenance mind-set soon chokes off evangelistic outreach. Before long, growth will slow and eventually cease.

As consultants, we had regularly seen this law in action. Most growing churches we had studied enjoyed growth patterns for three to ten years. However, a closer look at their growth rates revealed a gradual slowing. Eventually, growth would stop and maintenance would ensue. Once the maintenance mind-set had subtly worked its way into the church's philosophy, growth was effectively choked out of the life of the congregation.

Recognizing the tendency of maintenance to choke off growth is the first step toward arresting this ailment, but noticing its subtle onset is often difficult. The only procedure for identifying the onset of the choke law is to measure the tri-generational church's vital signs. As a doctor would not think of conducting a physical checkup without examining a patient's blood pressure, heartbeat, and temperature, so too there is a congregational vital sign that reveals the choke law's subtle approach. This vital sign is the measurement of numerical growth or decline, and the tool is accurate record keeping. Accurate record keeping should be the routine diagnostic tool among leaders of the Tri-Gen church the way a blood pressure gauge, stethoscope, and thermometer are the standard tools of a health provider's profession. "Measurement enables each congregation to monitor its own state of health. If it is not growing, something is wrong" write McGavran and Arn.[2]

Measuring a church's growth, or lack thereof, allows the church to implement tri- generational strategies, while keeping abreast of progress or regress. As mentioned in chapter 6, the Tri-Gen church model may not be suited to your situation. Although the Tri-Gen model may seem appropriate initially, how are leaders to know if it is appropriate in the long term? Measuring the church's growth is the best way to monitor suitability of the Tri-Gen model. In *Effective Evangelism: A Theological Mandate*, McGavran warns that leading a church without growth analysis is like working "blindfolded."[3]

The measurement of growth is an important antidote for exaggeration, as well, according to George Hunter. While analyzing the methods of John Wesley, Hunter noted, "Wesley had no interest in *puffed* statistics . . . (and) in reflecting on a case of the society in Dublin, he interpreted it as 'a warning to us all, how we give in to that hateful custom of painting things beyond life. Let us make a conscience of magnifying or exaggerating any thing. Let us rather speak under, than above, the truth. We, of all men, should be punctual in what we say; that none of our words may fall to the ground' (*Journal*, March 16, 1748)."[4] This punctuality of Wesley led to what Hunter calls a sanctified pragmatism, that included rigorous analysis of growth and decline within the Methodist societies. Hunter demonstrates again Wesley's meticulous approach by quoting this passage from Wesley's journal: "I returned to Norwich, and took an exact account of the society. I wish all our preachers would be accurate in their accounts, and rather speak under than above the truth. I had heard, again and again, of the increase of the society. And, what is the naked truth? Why, I left it 202 members; and I find 179. (March 21, 1779)."[5]

Four Types of Church Growth

If measurement of church growth is necessary to monitor the ongoing suitability of the tri-generational approach, how then is it to be conducted? Is growth merely a numbers game, counting heads like counting sheep? Hardly, for in actuality church growth is really comprised of four distinct types of growth, only one of which is numerical.

The nexus for understanding church growth is Acts 2:42-47. In this passage, the following four types of church growth are present.

Growing in Maturity

"They devoted themselves to the apostles' teaching and to the fellowship, to the breaking of bread and to prayer. Everyone was filled with awe, and many wonders and miraculous signs were done by the apostles" (Acts 2:42, 43). Immediately after the Holy Spirit's visitation at Pentecost, the young church drew together in a time of maturation growth. The significance of its members' devotion to teaching and fellowship, combined with the attesting miracles, testifies to a congregation maturing in its understanding and practice of spiritual principles.

Growing in Unity

"All the believers were together and had everything in common. Selling their possessions and goods, they gave to anyone, as he had need. Every day they continued to meet together in the temple courts. They broke bread in their homes and ate together with glad and sincere hearts, praising God..." (Acts 2:44-47a). The early church drew together in a unity and harmony that led to selfless acts of inter-reliance. Though pooling their money was not the norm for all, or even most, New Testament churches, unity, and interdependence is certainly a growth goal of all Christian communities. Unity and harmony create an atmosphere of mutual dependence and reciprocity, that bonds participants to the community and to their Lord.

Growing in Favor

"...and enjoying the favor of all the people" (Acts 2:47b). Church growth includes growth in testimony and respect among the unchurched people of the community. The result can be openness to the good news. Too often, however, an adversarial role develops between the church and the community. In reality, the role should be one of mutual respect, appreciation, and communication. When a church is meeting the felt needs of the community, as outlined in chapter 7, the church will receive the community's gratitude and acknowledgement. This gratitude then becomes a powerful conduit through which the good news flows into a community.

Growing in Numbers

"And the Lord added to their number daily those who were being saved" (v. 47c). The aftermath of the first three types of church growth is the last—growth in numerical size.

It is unfortunate that so many churches measure the last type of growth and ignore the first three. No accurate picture of the tri-generational church can take place without a careful study of *all* four types of church growth. The propensity to measure the latter is undoubtedly because it easily lends itself to statistical measurement. However, the authors have proposed several strategies for analyzing all four types of growth. But first let us briefly address a criticism that is often leveled against the practice of counting.

Is Counting Biblical?

Few principles in the church growth field have garnered as much controversy as the principle of measuring numerical growth. Donald McGavran counters that "the Church is made up of countable people and there is nothing particularly spiritual in not counting them. Men use the numerical approach in all worthwhile human endeavor."[6]

Some have argued that there *is* something spiritual about "not counting." They would point to God's displeasure with King David for ordering a census of the people in 1 Chronicles 21:1-30. However, 1 Chronicles 21:1 reveals that it was Satan who inspired David to conduct this counting of his troops. Even against the counsel of his commander, Joab, who discerned David's inappropriate motivation, David conducts the census. David's motivation for the census was to revel in the strength of his army, but God wanted David to put his trust in God's protection, rather than the size of his forces. Hence, wrong motivation and wrong instigation led to an inappropriate counting.

Elsewhere in the Bible, numberings are conducted for meaningful reasons with helpful results. In Numbers 1:2 and 26:2, God commands numberings of all Israel along with every segment of each tribe before and after the desert wanderings. In the Gospel accounts, we witness accurate countings of Jesus' team of disciples, and in Luke 10:1-24 we see a precise company of 72 disciples sent out two by two. In the parable of the lost sheep in Luke 15:3-7, only by counting the sheep does the shepherd become aware that one is missing from the fold. If counting those we are entrusted were odious to Jesus, certainly he would eliminate such imagery from his teaching. And, in Acts 1:15, 2:41, 4:4, Luke records the growth of the church by a careful record of its numerical increase. McGavran concludes "On biblical grounds, one has to affirm that devout use of the numerical approach is in accord with God's wishes. On the practical grounds, it is as necessary in congregations and denominations as honest financial dealing."[7]

Measuring Four Types of Growth

Growing in Maturity: Maturation Growth

The first three types of growth can be challenging to measure, due to their subjective nature. What is growth in maturity in one type of Tri-Gen congregation may not be in another. For example, a congregation with an emphasis on social action ministries might assess its maturation growth by counting the number of volunteers training for its philanthropic ministries. The number of people training for and carrying out ministries, such as a food shelf, clothing exchange, or homeless shelter might be a good indicator of people maturing in discipleship. However, in a tri-generational congregation emphasizing discipleship in small groups, calculating the number of people actively involved in the small group network might be a better method for ascertaining maturation growth.

However, there are some common categories of ministries within many Tri-Gen churches that can give a general assessment of growth in maturity; but first, let us define what we mean by maturation.

Jesus' Great Commission (Matthew 28:18-20) entrusts the church with a commission to "go and make disciples of all nations, baptizing them in the name of the Father and of the Son and of the Holy Spirit, and teaching them to obey everything I have commanded you." It is important to note that these actions—going, making disciples, baptizing, and teaching—are phrased in a manner that indicates an ongoing process. In addition, the sentence structure in the original Greek language emphasizes that "making disciples" is the central command of this commission. "Going," "baptizing," and "teaching" are parts of the process. As Wagner says, these latter actions are "never ends in themselves. They all should be used as a part of the process of making disciples."[8]

In addition, "making disciples" signifies that this learning must be an action that is continuing in the present. Thus, being a disciple is not just something one has completed in the past, but something that is happening presently, and that will continue in the future. R. V. G. Tasker points out that "the 'school days' of a Christian are never over."[9] Therefore, to count disciples, we look for ministries and programs in the tri-generational church that reveal that active learners are present.

Maturation growth may to a certain degree be measured by numbering a congregation's "active learners" who are regularly absorbing biblical lessons. Therefore, measuring the number of participants involved in educational and training opportunities can give an approximate idea of the active learners in a congregation. The statistic that totals the people involved in these areas we have labeled the "composite maturation number" (CMN). Figure 10.1 tells how to compute this aggregate number for your congregation.

The composite maturation growth should be recorded and then compared with subsequent years. Increase in this composite number signifies an increasing percentage of attendees involved in ongoing educational opportunities. Thus, computing this number can reveal a general idea if tri-generational strategies are producing active learners who are maturing in the principles and practices of Christianity.

Growing in Unity: Measuring Oneness

Growing in unity is another highly subjective area. A general idea of success can be determined through an analysis of how common identity, shared goals, and church-wide vision are developing among the different generations of the congregation. If a congregation can state and identify its tri-generational goals and vision, then unity is being shared at least intellectually among the different generational groupings. A congregational questionnaire is one of the best methods for uncovering this information.

In chapter 6, we saw in figure 6.5 how a congregation can

Figure 10.1

How to Compute Your
Composite Maturation Number (CMN)

Educational Opportunity Attendance (EOA):

1. **How many people are involved in**   EOA = _____
   educational opportunities per week?
   (Educational opportunities include
   Sunday school classes, cell groups
   with a learning format, Bible studies,
   Bible institutes, membership classes,
   newcomer classes, confirmation classes,
   classes in basic doctrine, or any gathering
   or class promoting Christian education.)

Average Attendance in Worship (AA):

2. **Compute the average attendance**   AA = _____
   per weekend.

Composite Maturation Number (CMN):

3. **To compute your maturation growth ratio**
   use the following formula:

_____   ÷   _____   =   _____
Your EOA (educational   Your AA (average   CMN
opportunity attendance)   attendance)   (Composite)
                                                         Maturation
                                                         Number*)

*The composite maturation number is read as a percent

---

establish its generational ratios with a simple congregational
questionnaire. To uncover growth in unity, it will be necessary to deploy a slightly more inclusive congregational questionnaire designed to uncover an understanding of shared
goals, vision, and identity.[10] Figure 10.2 gives an example of

congregational questions that can be asked to ascertain how pervasive intellectual unity is becoming in regards to goals, vision, and identity.

Figure 10.2

Please tell us when were you born.

Before 1946	1946–1964	1965–1983	1984 and after
___	___	___	___

Please check the box that represents the degree to which you agree or disagree with the following statements. Use the "do not know" box only if absolutely necessary.

	Agreement That Statement Describes You				
	Strong	Moderate	Slight	Disagree	Do Not Know
	(1)	(2)	(3)	(4)	(5)
1. If asked, I could roughly state for visitors and non-members, our church's *mission* statement.	❏	❏	❏	❏	❏
2. If asked, I could summarize in my own words for visitors and non-members, our church's *vision* statement.	❏	❏	❏	❏	❏
3. I have a sense of excitement about the future of our church.	❏	❏	❏	❏	❏
4. I have a clear understanding of the goals for our church.	❏	❏	❏	❏	❏

5. Our church feels like a network of individuals and age groups with the same goals, but with different expressions.	❏	❏	❏	❏	❏
6. Combined worship services (unity services) are highly valued in our church.	❏	❏	❏	❏	❏
7. Though we are a network of individuals and age groups, we have a unified identity in the community.	❏	❏	❏	❏	❏

In figure 10.2, questions 1, 2, and 3 deal with the degree to which a common vision is understood and embraced. Questions 4 and 5 address whether shared goals are present. Questions 6 and 7 assess the degree to which common identity is exhibited.

A congregational questionnaire is most effective when given at all church celebrations, twice a year on two consecutive weekends. On the second weekend, it is important to ask those who have taken the questionnaire the week before not to take it again. The questionnaire should be compared with earlier questionnaires to determine growth in shared goals, vision, and identity. If, over time, there is an increase in the numerical outcome on the questions of Figure 10.2, it should be obvious that, at the very least, mental assent to unifying factors is increasing.

Another gauge of unity is participation in "unity" services. In chapter 8, we described how to host a periodic unity celebration. This combined worship event is a celebration of one Lord among different generations. Attendance at unity events can be another indicator of emerging unity.

However, the Tri-Gen congregation must not expect

attendance at this combined celebration to equal exactly the combined total of individual generation-specific celebrations. As noted earlier, worship is a highly individualized and personal activity. Some attendees at the parallel worship celebrations may not like the blended format of the unity celebration. Therefore, it is not wise to gauge success based upon the degree to which the unity service attendance equals the combined attendance of the individual celebrations. For example, it would be imprudent to expect that a church with a Builder celebration of 120, a Boomer celebration of 175, and a Gen-X celebration of 90 would garner 385 attendees at a unity service. A more realistic number might be 250 from these three worship expressions. In addition, unity services tend to attract a higher percentage of guests. Another 30 to 50 guests might be expected to bring the total to nearly 300. However, this is still short of the 385 that might be erroneously expected.

Therefore, due to these variables, compare the attendance numbers of a unity celebration only against earlier unity celebrations. Comparing proverbial apples to apples exposes a healthier picture of unity growth.

Growing in Favor: Measuring Community Awareness

Growing in favor indicates the extent to which a church is establishing and maintaining a positive image and mutual respect in the community. Data gathering will take place in a manner similar to the process employed with the community survey in chapter 7. As mentioned earlier, though the door-to-door interview has been popular, it has fallen into some disfavor. The telephone interview has subsequently emerged as less intrusive than the face-to-face visit.

Figure 10.3 gives sample questions that may be used for a community awareness survey.

Do not forget to call only at a convenient time. Do not call during meals or late in the evening. Figure 7.7 in chapter 7 reveals the best times to call are evenings between 6:30 and

Figure 10.3

Telephone Community Awareness Survey

Introduction

"Hello. My name is _____(name)_____ and I am conducting a short survey for _____(name of congregation)_____ in _____(city/town)_____. Would you mind if I asked you a few anonymous and short questions?"

- If "YES" continue.
- If "NO" conclude by saying "thank you for your consideration, good-bye."

Survey Parameters

"We are undertaking a study of different generations in our community. Were you born..."

❏ In 1984 or more recently?
❏ In or between the years of 1965 to 1983?
❏ In or between the years of 1964 to 1946?
❏ In or between the years of 1927 to 1945?
❏ In or before 1926?

Open-ended Questions

Question #1: "Are you aware of _(name of congregation)_ in _(city/town)_ ?" If *yes* continue. If *no* conclude interview by saying, "that concludes our interview. Thank you for your time. Good-bye."

Question #2: "How would you describe this church to a friend?"

Question #3: "In general, do you have a positive, negative or undecided view of this church?"

Question #4: "What advice could you give this church so it could more effectively help people in your age group?"

Question #5: "Are you currently actively involved in a church, synagogue, mosque, or other religious house of worship?"

Conclusion

"Thank you for your time. Your advice will help _(name of congregation)_ of _(city/town)_ better address the needs of people in our community(ies). Thank you. Good-bye."

9:00 P.M., Saturdays from 10:00 A.M. to 4:00 P.M. and Sundays from noon to 9:00 P.M.

The rule of thumb for the minimum number of calls needed in a community awareness survey is that 0.3 percent of the total population should be sampled. Therefore, if 50,000 people live within a twenty-minute drive[11] of your congregation, a good sample would be 150 telephone calls.

Following guidelines similar to those for the Need Assessment Questionnaire of chapter 7, begin a five-phase process to correlate your responses to the telephone calls.

(1) Write down short phrases that summarize the response that you are receiving. (See figure 10.4).

(2) Immediately upon completion of all interviews, interviewers should review the responses and rank "key words" in frequency. See figure 10.4 again for an example of how this may be accomplished.

Figure 10.4

Question Responses	Key Words
Friendly church with a good youth program	• Friendly • Youth program
Music is important	• Music
Involved in a food shelf, Habitat for Humanity, and a women's shelter	• Food shelf • Habitat for Humanity • Women's shelter
After school care for school age children, with a youth choir	• Kid's Club • Youth Choir

(3) Next, all interviewers should compare their results, looking for common responses and key words.

(4) All interviewers should compile a list of key words and phrases that describe, in order of frequency, the perspective people have about this congregation.

(5) Finally, convene all interviewers to correlate their responses. Go over the following:

• Are their common key words found?

• Classify key words into two groups: positive and negative.

• Next, two options for analyzing and comparing these key words may be used.

    a. With the group, prioritize the key words by frequency and list the top ten positive and negative key words. Compare your lists of ten annually.

    b. With your group, count the number of times certain words (or their synonyms) appear. Do this for both positive and negative words, separately. For example "unfriendly" or its synonyms ("cold," "cool," "aloof," "indifferent," "detached" or "indifferent") might decrease in frequency from 32 citations in year one of the survey, to less than ten in year two.

Growing in Numbers: Attendance Growth

Evaluating your numerical growth begins with accurate recording keeping, but, what type of numerical records will be kept? This is an important question, for a haphazard or inaccurate counting will lead to confusion and distortion. Even terminology must be monitored. Donald McGavran observed that "baptized believers" can mean "adult baptized believers in good standing" for a Church of Christ congregation, and "all the baptized, infants and adults" in an Episcopal congregation. Thus, the Episcopal church would appear larger than the Church of Christ's, even if, in actuality, the opposite were true.[12] As a result, measuring membership is not a good universal barometer of church growth. Instead, church attendance can give a more accurate picture of church growth or decline. To evaluate your attendance growth, you must undertake a three-step process.

STEP 1

Determine whether or not you will count children. Children will skew the data in favor of congregations with large families. And, since determining age is difficult, it is almost impossible to count only adults when counting heads during a church service. For example, if a congregation wished to count everyone 13 years and older, the counters would have a difficult task determining if a person was 12 or 13 while counting from the back or balcony of a church sanctuary. Some congregations have solved this by counting the congregation after the children have been dismissed for a children's sermon or children's church. In order not to risk missing adults who are working with the children at this time, congregations then send counters to the children's activity rooms to count adult volunteers. This is a moderately effective way to count these adults. However, because of the difficulties involved, many congregations will opt for counting adults and children in attendance. Whichever process is adopted, it is important to be consistent. A good determining factor will be to investigate what the church has done in the past.

STEP 2

Determine your past Average Annual Growth Rate (AAGR). The AAGR is your net increase or decrease in church attendance over a period of years. (Figure 10.5 demonstrates how to compute your AAGR, as well as how to compute your annual growth rate (AGR). The AGR is used for comparing data between two consecutive years.)

Figure 10:5

How to Compute Your
Average Annual Growth Rate (AAGR)*

_____ − _____ ÷ _____ ÷ _____ X 100 = _____

This year's membership /attendance figure	Your *base* membership /attendance figure	Your *base* membership /attendance figure	Number of years being examined	**AAGR**
	(i.e., the first year for the period you are studying)	↑ ←These are the same numbers.		This is read as a percent of annual growth.

How to Compute Your
Annual Growth Rate (AGR)**

_____ − _____ ÷ _____ = _____

This year's membership /attendance figure	Last year's membership /attendance figure	Last year's membership /attendance figure	**AAGR**
		↑ ↑ ←These are the same numbers.	This is read as a percent of annual growth.

*Use the average annual growth rate (AAGR) when you are seeking an average over a period of years, i.e., when analyzing your past figures.
**Use the annual growth rate (AGR) if you are comparing two consecutive years, in order to obtain yearly comparisons to be used to predict future growth.

Computing your AAGR will ensure that large numbers do not skew your data. For example, an average small church of 100 attendees might grow to 200 in five years. A large-sized church of 500 might grow to 600 in the same period. Using Figure 10.5, we can compute that the small church has an average annual growth rate of 20 percent, while the larger church has an AAGR of only 4 percent. Both have added 100 members, but the smaller church has grown faster.

STEP 3

Annually track your annual growth rate (AGR) to ascertain growth or decline. Display this information prominently with a chart or graph. Furthermore, provide copies to leaders and make sure it is visable in areas where planning is done.

For recording attendance, there are two methods worth considering.

- To maintain the highest degree of accuracy, count every Sunday in order to yield a yearly average.
- However, some congregations prefer a sampling method, where the congregation is counted approximately four times a year. This method requires less effort, and can yield results almost as accurate as those of the every weekend method. Small churches may find this approach easier to conduct with their limited person power. At other times, the sheer size of larger congregations may require this. However, to maintain accuracy in the sampling method, it is important to keep several guidelines in mind. First, sample four *typical* weekends each year. Exclude holidays, church events, special guests, and any unusual factors. Be sure to count at the same time each year. The best times are once between late September and early November; again between mid-January and early March; again between late April (after Easter) and before the end of May; and finally, once over the summer, in June or July.

Monitor Generational Ratios

In Your Community

In chapter 7, we saw how census data can reveal the generational ratios within the sphere of influence of your church. Return to this chapter, if you need to review how to gather and use the data available from the U. S. Census Bureau. It is important that you yearly monitor the ratios of all generations in your community. A community's generational ratios will provide the goal that a healthy Tri-Gen church will attempt to mirror proportionally in congregational makeup.

In Your Church

At the same time, it is important to monitor generational ratios in your congregation. A simple questionnaire such as the one suggested in figure 6.5, can be administered one to four times a year. The sampling guidelines from above can be applied here to ensure the sampling of generational ratios is accurate. In addition, use figure 10.6 to contrast the changes in your generational ratios.

Goals and Timelines

The goal of the evaluation process is to grow among all three generations, and to do so in a generational ratio that approximates the ratio present in the community. Only by an ongoing analysis of community generational ratios, church ratios, and church growth patterns will evaluation be adequate to gauge true numerical growth.

In addition, a timeline must be employed. An old adage is that "if you don't have a target, then you are sure to miss it." For each congregation, the time limit will vary. Most large congregations (401+ members) are discovering that three years is the minimum time needed to grow into a healthy tri-generational format. Medium-sized congregations (201–400 in regular attendance) have discovered that four years is typical. Surprisingly, the flexibility of small-sized congregations

219

Figure 10.6

COMPARING CHANGES IN GENERATIONAL
PERCENTAGES (GP)

	YEAR 1		YEAR 2		YEAR 3		YEAR 4		YEAR 5	
Birth Years	No.	%*	No.	%	No.	%	No.	%	No.	%
1965–1983 **Gen X**										
1964–1946 **Boomers**										
1945 and before **Builders**										

*To discover your generational percentage (GP) of each age group, divide the number of attendees (or members) in each age group by the total membership. For example:

Number of attendees/ of each age group	÷	Total membership	=	**GP** Generational Percentage of a particular age group

(200 or fewer attendees) has allowed them to be the quickest to adopt the Tri-Gen model. Many churches under 200 attendees are making the move to the tri-generational format in a minimum of two years. However, in most cases, these are minimums. When the alternative of a slow decline and eventual closure is considered, the energy and time required pale in comparison. Establishing deadlines is the only way to ensure that time and energies are not squandered. Eddie Gibbs, in his dry English humor, sums this up nicely, "When there are no deadlines, most of us are tempted to extend our lines indefinitely."[13]

The Significance of Evaluation

Evaluation is the fundamental tool that keeps practitioners abreast of progress. Consequently, a natural aversion among church leaders toward exaggeration and/or ignorance regarding numbers must be curtailed at once. The suspicion and cynicism that have been the flotsam and jetsam of our statistical phobia must be quickly abandoned. It is time the church recognizes that its ability effectively to carry out the Great Commission depends upon an accurate assessment of those methodologies that demonstrate God's hand of blessing. The church seeking to attain a healthy and contagious tri-generational personality must be willing to evaluate progress or regress openly, diligently, and accurately.

We've Almost Arrived at the Most Important Step of All

Now that we have completed six steps, the final step is before us. This step, which we shall cover in the next chapter, is the most crucial step of all. This is the role prayer plays in reaching people. Because it is the Holy Spirit that draws people to Christ and His church, prayer becomes the cornerstone of our strategy. George Hunter concisely addresses this dynamic when he entreats

> Pray to be led to receptive people.... We are not teaching a nonspiritual technology for evangelism. Indeed, such is not possible because evangelism is the Holy Spirit's work at every point: he prepares those who he desires to call; he prepares and leads those who he sends out; and if receptive people sense his approach through our outreach, and respond in faith—this, too, is his work.[14]

221

Chapter Eleven

STEP 7: Mobilizing Your Church for Transgenerational Prayer

Why Is Prayer Step 7?

Now that you have been introduced to the mechanics of the tri-generational model, it is time to cover a step for which there is no peer. It is this stage which energizes all others. The reader should not be misled by our allocating it to Step 7, for in our opinion it has the utmost effect upon all outcomes. It is the power of prayer.

A valid question might be, "If prayer is so critical, why is it relegated to Step 7 in a seven-step process?" Recall that earlier, we suggested that *all* steps must be fully investigated and understood before any individual step is undertaken. We have chosen to conclude our system with prayer, so that the reader will possess an educated focus for his or her prayers. It is our firm conviction that each component of the seven steps must be bathed in prayer. The envisioning process will only take hold if sincere prayer is attached. The ability to identify the needs of the unchurched will be achieved only when prayer is part of the process. Worship in the trigenerational format will only break forth if accompanied by passionate prayer. Each step of the seven-step process requires prayer by the participants, prayer by the church, and prayer among those gifted in intercessory prayer.

Is Prayer Really Necessary for Church Growth?

John 16:8, 9 clearly states that only the Holy Spirit can convict of sin, call to repentance, and convert people to Christ. Therefore, prayer becomes a believer's highest priority. A popular maxim is that "prayer is the right arm of evangelism."

In fact, great church growth has historically coincided with great church prayer. The phenomenal church growth witnessed in the book of Acts can be traced to the disciples' dedication to corporate prayer (Acts 4:23-31, 6:4, and 12:5). John Wesley, who helped turn the spiritual tides in England back to Christ said, "All of God's works are done through believing prayer."[1] Dwight L. Moody, the American lay evangelist who "shook two continents for God"[2] is often remembered for his observation that "every work of God can be traced to some kneeling form."[3] William E. Sangster, well-known Methodist leader during the first half of the twentieth century said, "Passionate, pleading, persistent prayer is always the prelude to revival."[4] Dr. Billy Graham has suggested that, "The secret of each Crusade has been the power of God's Spirit moving in answer to the prayers of His people. I have often said that the three most important things we can do for a Crusade is to pray, to pray, and to pray."[5] In *I Believe in Church Growth*, Eddie Gibbs concludes that, "As one studies case histories of growing churches, there is one recurring factor—they are all *praying* churches" (italics his).[6]

Therefore, to commence a journey toward a Tri-Gen church without a strong and an expansive prayer base is not only foolhardy, but also is somewhat presumptuous. Gibbs cautions that, "No matter how helpful some of the tools presented (in his book) seem to appear, they will prove useless and even harmful if taken up by those with eyes that are spiritually blind and whose hands lack spiritual strength."[7] Prayer is God's chosen process for enlightening and strengthening His people. To launch any endeavor without extended deliberation with God is ill advised.

223

Methods for Mobilizing Prayer

Refocus the Prayer Meeting with 50/50 Prayer

Weekly prayer meetings are customary in many churches. Usually, they have been inaugurated years earlier by a Builder generation well acquainted with the power of prayer. In many churches, this prayer meeting will be held on a week night or a Sunday evening. In format, it will often resemble a small church service. It may include songs, testimonials, a few announcements, numerous prayer requests, and an extended time of prayer. In many churches, this prayer meeting is comprised primarily of the Builders. Because of the songs, the format, and the attendees, the meeting will frequently possess a Builder personality.

The focus of prayer meetings is usually the needs of congregational members. While some prayers will be offered for societal issues, as well as for the unchurched, the great majority of time will address the needs of those within the church. A helpful exercise is to tabulate the number of prayer requests tendered for the unchurched with the number offered for the church. Usually, it is discovered that upwards of 80 percent of the prayers will be focused on existing members, their families, and their friends. Prayer for the unchurched to come to know Christ will usually be less than 20 percent. James 4:2 warns that neglected prayer results in unanswered requests. Jesus admonished in John 4:35*b* to "open your eyes and look at the fields! They are ripe for harvest."

There is nothing wrong with prayer for the people of God, and the authors do not wish to diminish it in any way. However, the implications of the above scriptures are that if evangelism is to occur, then prayer meetings must include a significant amount of prayer for the unchurched. In fairness, it would seem that our prayer meetings should be refocused to allow 50 percent of the time for prayer for church members, and another 50 percent of the time directed toward the unchurched. This we call "50/50 prayer."

To employ this 50/50 prayer balance, we are *not* suggesting that prayer time be shortened. Reducing the amount of time given to prayer, or the amount of prayers offered for the church, would be misguided. Rather, we are suggesting that our prayer meetings be *lengthened* to allow a 50/50 prayer format. For example, a 60-minute time of prayer might include nearly 50 minutes of prayer for the church body, and roughly 10 minutes for the unchurched. Think of the power that could be released, if the meeting was refocused by praying 50 minutes for the church's needs, and another 50 minutes for the needs of the unchurched. James 4:2 and John 4:35*b* seem to imply that church growth and health would result.

Utilize Concerts of Prayer for Boomers and Gen-Xers

In many cases, the Builder-oriented prayer meeting has been the spiritual powerhouse of the congregation. Though open to all generations, its Builder personality may have unintentionally made it less attractive to Boomers and Generation X. To change its format, songs and formalities would significantly alter its personality and estrange the Builders that attend. Therefore, it is better to start something similar, but new.

The early 1980s witnessed a new approach to the prayer meeting called "concerts of prayer." David Bryant, former missions specialist with Inter-Varsity Christian Fellowship, popularized this reworking of the prayer meeting. Among Boomers and Generation X, variations of the format caught on.

The term "concert" struck a chord with younger generations accustomed to musical concerts. Bryant reclaimed the term "concert" from Jesus' promise in Matthew 18:19 that "...if two of you on earth agree about anything you ask for, it will be done for you by my Father in heaven." The Greek word for "agree" is *sumphoneo* and means "to be in agreement, in harmony."[8] From this Greek word, the English word "symphony" is derived. So, *agreeing* together can be thought of as praying in symphony or "concert" to God. Bryant defined these concerts of prayer as, "A movement of prayer ...a coalition of praying people who regularly unite for a very specific agenda surrounding spiritual awakening and world evangelism."[9]

Concerts of prayer were best known for the large gatherings held in stadiums and arenas. But, the legacy of this movement is the smaller concerts and miniconcerts that developed within the local church. Some churches host a concert of prayer once a month for two hours. Other congregations employ thirty-minute miniconcerts after each worship service. Still other congregations opt for fifteen-minute microconcerts after committee meetings and fellowship gatherings.

The format for these concerts of prayer is similar to an updated Builder prayer meeting. In the concert format, praise choruses are intermingled with testimonies, small group prayer time, and corporate prayer for the needs of both the church and the unchurched. Among the Builder generation, the term "concert" has been a bit unsettling, but the Boomers and Gen-Xers, raised with the idea of a concert as an event, quickly embraced the idea.

Planning a concert of prayer includes six ingredients, which are often moved around to prevent monotony and tedium. Thus, although concerts of prayer differ greatly, most will include the following.

1. PRAYER FOR THE UNCHURCHED

Participants are often encouraged to visualize their friends, relatives, associates, and neighbors (F.R.A.Ns) who are unchurched or in need of Christ. They are encouraged to pray for them by name. Sometimes, concert participants will stand and face varying points of the compass in order to pray for the unchurched people who live to the north, the south, the east, and the west.

2. PRAYER FOR CHRISTIANS

Meeting the needs of believers is an important part of the concert approach. Often, these personal needs are shared in small groups that are established at the concerts. A 50/50 prayer ratio (for Christians, as well as the unchurched) is readily found in concerts of prayer.

3. CORPORATE, LARGE GROUP PRAYER

At times, this approach draws together all participants to pray corporately for the needs both inside and outside the church. This is an element that can enhance identity and unity, as well as releasing spiritual power.

4. ONE-ON-ONE AND SMALL GROUP PRAYER

Two of the enduring benefits of the concert of prayer movement is one-on-one prayer, as well as prayer within small "huddle" groups. Concert participants first form partners for one-on-one prayer. Next, they combine three sets of partners to form a "huddle." This approach fosters intimacy, camaraderie, and emotional closeness. Here, too, accountability is nurtured, as participants are encouraged to report to one another after the concert when prayers are answered.

5. TESTIMONIES

Declarations of personal triumphs achieved through prayer have the effect of encouraging more prayer. Concerts of prayer include testimonials from participants and leaders about the power and potency of prayer.

6. MUSIC

Concerts of prayer employ praise choruses to encourage a time of corporate worship. The use of music, and its frequency, is similar to how hymns are employed in a Builder-oriented prayer meeting. But, in a concert of prayer, the music is updated and culture-current.

As mentioned earlier, each concert of prayer may contain a different mixture of the above components. A miniconcert of prayer that might take place after a worship service could be organized like the example in figure 11.1.

227

Figure 11.1

Miniconcert of Prayer
(30 minutes)

- Celebration (10 minutes). Two worship choruses begin the miniconcert.

- Preparation (5 minutes). This is a short overview on the focus of the praying. Partners are chosen and huddles are formed.

- Dedication (5 minutes). Here, the attendees confess sin and commit to be servants of prayer.

- One-on-one prayer (5 minutes). Attendees pray with their partner.

- Small group prayer (5 minutes). Three sets of partners form a huddle for prayer. The event leader might help guide this time by offering suggestions for prayer from the lectern.

A two-hour concert of prayer held once a month could resemble figure 11.2.

Times for hosting concerts of prayer can include (but are not limited to):

(1) Before or after church.
(2) Before or after committee meetings.
(3) At various times during the week or month.
(4) Before or after church events.
(5) Before or after public events hosted by the church.
(6) Before, during, or after evangelistic meetings or ventures.

Figures 11.1 and 11.2 are for illustration only. The actual format of a concert or miniconcert of prayer can be as varied

Figure 11.2

Full Concert of Prayer
(2 hours)

- Celebration (15 minutes). The meeting begins with three worship choruses.

- Preparation (20 minutes). A welcome is followed by a biblical perspective prayer. Partners are chosen and huddles are formed.

- Dedication (5 minutes). Here, the attendees confess sin and commit to be servants of prayer.

- Awakening: Prayer for Body of Christ (30 minutes). This portion of the concert begins with prayer among personal partners, then continues in huddles, and finally draws everyone together to pray in unison.

- Mission: Prayer for the unchurched (30 minutes). This also starts with personal partners, then moves into huddles, and finally joins together corporately.

- Two Testimonies (10 minutes). One testimony is given on the awakening theme, and the other addresses the mission theme.

- Conclusion (10 minutes). This finale focuses on the attendees' commitment to be used in any way God may choose. It starts with prayer between partners, then moves into huddles, and finally concludes with prayers of praise along with a praise chorus.

---

as the venue, the participants, and the theme. The important distinction is that a concert of prayer includes the contemporary choruses, small group interaction, and variety that is attractive to both Boomers and Generation X.

Organize Prayer Triplets

The idea of this innovative approach is to meet regularly with two Christian friends to pray for seven to ten unchurched F.R.A.Ns. This strategy was popularized by the Billy Graham Evangelistic Association, in conjunction with their crusades. The use of three people led to these unpretentious prayer networks being christened "prayer triplets."

The small number of participants offers flexibility. Prayer triplets can easily be convened at work, perhaps during a break or over lunch. At other times, prayer triplets will be held in homes, in schools, in restaurants, or even while commuting.

Prayer triplets customarily meet once a week, though this is not decreed. However, regularity is important. Moreover, with the conference call feature available from most telephone companies today, it is easy to convene these prayer triplets over the telephone. The proliferation of the Internet also allows e-mail and chat rooms to be environments in which the prayer triplet can thrive.

The simplicity of the prayer triplet is carried into the agenda, which creates a reciprocal and reoccurring environment for prayer. Figure 11.3 offers suggestions on how to organize and conduct a prayer triplet.

The straightforwardness and flexibility of the prayer triplet makes it a highly effective tool for establishing social networks with a prayer focus.

Deploy Neighborhood Prayer Groups

Neighborhood prayer groups are geographically distributed small groups that pray for unchurched people living nearby. Sometimes they will pray over a map, or undertake a prayer trek around the neighborhood. This group is distinguished by a burden; not only for the unchurched, but also for the community in which they reside. They will usually meet once a week, and sometimes more often. Their

Figure 11:3

Creating a Prayer Triplet[10]

1. Choose two Christian friends, relatives, associates, or neighbors (F.R.A.Ns).

2. Agree on a weekly time to meet in person, on the telephone, or over the Internet. Ideally, this should be at least 10 minutes in length.

3. Each person shares the names of at least three people who do not attend church.

4. Pray silently and aloud for these people, and for each other in your relationship with them.

5. Pray for their personal needs, their families, and their openness to Christ and His church.

6. Pray for your pastor and your church.

---

gatherings are customarily structured along steps 2 to 6 of the prayer triplet as described in figure 11.3. The difference between prayer triplets and neighborhood prayer groups is that the latter are larger, about the size of a cell group (3 to 12 people). In addition, the meeting of the neighborhood prayer group will usually include testimonies and worship, so it often reflects the structure of the miniconcert of prayer.

Make a "Bridges of God" List

This approach uses a card bearing a "bridges of God" or "prayer covenant list" of seven to ten people who are presently not attending a church. The card can be any size, but the most popular is the size of a bookmark that can be easily carried in a Bible, billfold, or purse. Figure 11.4 gives an example of a bridges of God list.

Figure 11.4

Prayer Covenant List

1. _____

2. _____

3. _____

4. _____

5. _____

6. _____

7. _____

"Andrew...went straight off and found his brother Simon...and brought him to Jesus." John 1:40-42 (JBP)

The card bearers promise or covenant to pray daily for those listed on the card. In these prayers, they ask God to give them opportunities to cross the bridges of relationships, and invite these persons to church. The Billy Graham Evangelistic Association employs a version it calls "Operation Andrew," so named because it was Andrew who in John 1:40-42 went and found his brother Simon Peter and brought him to Jesus.

The Billy Graham Evangelistic Association has suggested four attitudes that will enhance success with such lists.[11] These attitudes include:

(1) Look around—because your mission field is right where you live, work, and go to school.

(2) Look up—for prayer changes people.

(3) Look out—for ways to cultivate friendship and earn the confidence of those on your list.

(4) Look after—those who respond to Christ; they need your encouragement more than ever. Those who do not come at once may be reached later, so continue to love them and pray.

Many churches have experienced dramatic success by distributing these cards to church attendees five to six weeks before a combined "unity service." The unity service provides an opportunity for parishioners to invite their F.R.A.Ns. Distributing these cards in advance allows the congregant multiple opportunities to pray for, as well as invite, their potential guests. The law of multiple invitations suggests that a bridges of God list may be a good way to remind people to pray for and invite their F.R.A.Ns continually and tenaciously.

Discover Your "Bridge of God" Person

Some congregations may be uneasy with, or unaccustomed to, using such a long list. Whether through bad experiences in the past, or a perceived marketing nature to the list, some congregations shy away from using the bridges of God list.

However, these churches need not abandon this approach entirely. Donald McGavran recounts how one church grew from 40 members to more than 220 when each church member focused prayer on only *one* unchurched person.[12] The church was a member of a network made up of 23 small town congregations. All but one church was stagnated. The lone growing church was in a stable community, and it was evident that community growth was not fueling the church's expansion. McGavran discovered that each January, this growing congregation asked each member to select from among his or her friends, relatives, associates, and neighbors one person who appeared most likely to respond. The church member then prayed daily for that person.

McGavran recalls that the pastor often publicly prayed for "our friends for whom each of us is praying." Though only one person was selected per congregant, the result was meaningful church growth. McGavran noted that there arose "a keen consciousness of being God's instrument in the salvation of scores of their own best friends and loved ones." He concluded that this was "one of the most effective plans to come to my attention, and one which could be used in congregations in the United States and every other nation."[13] Looking across the bridges of God and reaching just one person is a reasonable and rewarding way to connect with the unchurched.

Liberate Your Intercessors

C. Peter Wagner suggested in *Your Spiritual Gifts Can Help Your Church Grow* that there is an often overlooked, but crucial, gift that the church needs to stimulate growth. This is the gift of intercessory prayer. People possessing this gift feel an unusually strong desire to pray for extended periods of time. In addition, they see specific and frequent answers to their prayers. Their prayers do not replace the prayers that each Christian is responsible to lift before God; but they add a new dimension to prayer, by offering prayer that, as Wagner describes, "...involves a combination of identification, agony, and authority that those without the gift can seldom if ever experience, or even identify with."[14]

Many growing churches have discovered, developed, and deployed people with this gift, releasing them to pray for the unchurched. Some congregations have hired full-time intercessors to fulfill this important duty. Wagner muses, "If prayer is as important as we all think it is, I find it curious that churches do not hire staff members to give themselves to intercession—staff is hired for just about everything else."[15] Happily, many Christian organizations are recognizing the potency of prayer offered by professional intercessors. Since the 1970s, Campus Crusade for Christ has assigned certain staff members to intercede full time for the organization's evangelistic efforts.

Whether full-time employees or part-time volunteers, utilizing men and women with the gift of intercessory prayer will unleash the strategies and systems discussed in this book. In addition, using those with the gift of intercessory prayer allows our seven steps to have their full effect upon both the secular community and Christ's church.

Prayer Teams

Similar in composition to the Neighborhood Prayer Center, but without a geographic orientation, is the prayer team approach. This is a team designated to pray regularly for unchurched people. Sometimes these teams will be convened during a specific evangelistic endeavor or activity. But, most often, these teams will be year-round contingents of three to twelve people.

As can be seen from the preceding discussion, these teams will be the most effective if comprised of intercessors. Often, they will meet concurrently with evangelistic activities, such as unity services or community surveys. When Coral Ridge Presbyterian Church used intercessory teams in conjunction with its Evangelism Explosion program, Wagner reports that it encountered a 100 percent increase in professions of faith.[16]

Due to their small group character, prayer teams are flexible enough to meet at various times and pray specifically for diverse needs. The prayer team format also gives those with the gifts of intercession the mutual support and encouragement they need to offer regular, focused, lengthy, and effective prayer.

Prayer Places—Make Room to Pray

When Terry Teykl, pastor of Aldersgate United Methodist Church, returned from South Korea, he was a changed man. He was always what many would call a man of prayer and the congregation that he pastored had a strong prayer emphasis. But, in Korea, he was surprised and overwhelmed by the way Korean Christians were dedicated to prayer. At one countryside retreat, he witnessed tiny prayer "grottos" where hundreds came to pray daily.

After returning to America, Teykl experienced a growing passion to see all churches have a room designated specifically for prayer. He encouraged churches to set aside prayer rooms that would cultivate and encourage prayer. Teykl's book, *Making Room to Pray*, recounts the phenomenal spiritual and physical growth churches have experienced after developing such prayer rooms.[17]

Prayer rooms come in all configurations, but the key ingredient is that they are designed to promote extended and fervent prayer. In his book, *Blueprint for the House of Prayer*, Teykl suggests prayer places customarily maintain five characteristics.[18] The following are these characteristics, elaborated upon by the present authors.

(1) *A prayer place is private.* They can be small rooms, large rooms, unused offices, portable buildings, empty storage closets, and chapels. They can be almost anything as long as they are designed to minimize outside distractions. Such venues give the person praying a cloistered environment, which filters out extraneous diversions.

(2) *A prayer place is comfortable.* Some people stand when they pray, others prostrate themselves, and many kneel. The comfortable nature of a prayer place is not designed to promote absent-mindedness, or even sleep, but to reduce the distractions and discomforts that hinder concentration.

(3) *A prayer place is inspirational and informative.* Prayer places employ materials to help persons focus on prayer. Maps, pictures, clocks (to note the time around the world), literature on unreached people, names of local officials, newspaper clippings, and names of community caregivers help focus prayer.

(4) *A prayer place is accessible 24 hours a day.* This often requires a well lit outside entrance and a telephone. Because iniquity does not wane in the night, neither should prayer.

(5) *A prayer place is staffed as much as possible.* One goal is to have prayer volunteers praying around the clock in the prayer room. This can be attained by scheduling church volunteers in one-to-four hour segments. The objective is to offer effective and continuous prayer.

Establishing prayer places has become an excellent strategy for focusing prayer within a congregation. Creating a definite and dedicated room for prayer stresses the primacy of prayer in the congregational milieu. And, after all, reworking a phrase from Wagner, "We have rooms for just about everything else."

It Is Time to Elevate Prayer

In our diagnostic analysis of churches, we have found that prayer is probably the least organized, minimally funded, and overlooked ministry in the Body of Christ. Yet, we have seen that prayer plays a strategic role in the travel of the good news across the bridges of God. If we intend to take seriously the Great Commission (Matthew 28:18-20), then it is time we elevate prayer to its rightful place in our churches with the same organizational and financial status as other key ministries.

EPILOGUE

Which Church Will Yours Be in the 21st Century?

An Unhealthy Model—The One-Generation Church

The church of the twenty-first century will evolve into two distinct and very different models. Most churches, perhaps up to 85 percent, will slowly mutate into generational polarization. They will become one-generation enclaves. And, as their primary generation ages, due to geriatrophy, they will die.

The one-generational church is far different from the church of even fifty years ago. In the last century, the close proximity of extended families forced churches to remain multigenerational. Sadly, today this controlling force has dissipated.

Tri-Gen Congregations: Holistic and Healthy

A second model will continue to rise during the next century, and it will be healthier than the first. It will embrace, and even foster, generational distinctiveness. Though it may always be a minority among all churches, it will be a healthier and more enduring one. It will be the tri-generational church.

The tri-generational church will foster an environment where three distinct generational sub-congregations peacefully coexist under one roof, one name, and one leadership team. It will bring intergenerational mentoring, experience, and understanding back to the church. In an increasingly fragmented society, the church may become the one reliable venue where multiple generations intersect regularly. The Tri-Gen church is the holistic and healthy model of the future. The tri-generational church makes sense from both an anthropological and a biblical perspective.

The Tri-Gen Church Makes...

Biblical Sense

The multigenerational congregation was the normative expression for the church in biblical times. Paul's entreaty to a youthful Titus to foster sound doctrine by "teaching the older women to be reverent in the way they live...Then they can train the younger women..." (Titus 2:3*a*, 4*a*) presupposes a multigenerational milieu. In Titus 2:2, Paul's exhortation to older men certainly assumes they will be examples to younger believers. The Bible is replete with examples that presume a multigenerational church.

Anthropological Sense

The tri-generational church makes sense anthropologically, as well. As Margaret Mead observed, "The continuity of all cultures depends on the living presence of at least three generations."[1] Values of integrity, morality, and religious faith are best passed down when grandchild interacts and interfaces regularly with grandparent. It is across these intergenerational conduits that cultural values and convictions most readily travel.

How Is This to Be Accomplished?

Seven Steps to Soundness

How is a healthy Tri-Gen model to be inaugurated? In the preceding chapters, we saw that it most naturally unfolds when implemented in seven steps.

(Step 1) The process begins by envisioning the leadership, church, and community (in that order) with the necessity and longevity of the tri-generational model. Envisioning begins by asking ourselves, "Who are we, uniquely?" (our *philosophy of ministry*) and "What do we do?" (our *mission* statement). The envisioning process then reaches its apogee when we discover, "Where do we believe God is calling our church to go in the future?" (our *vision* statement).

(Step 2) Our next step is to foster a degree of autonomy by developing parallel committees to oversee generational ministries. Worship celebrations, Christian education, small group networks, and evangelistic outreaches are but a few of the areas where specific generational ministries will flourish. Parallel committees work concurrently overseeing these ministries for different generations. In addition, unified and executive committees address common concerns and maintain accountability.

(Step 3) Next, we discover the felt needs among those generations missing from our congregations. Surveying people who live and work in close proximity to ourselves unleashes a wealth of information on the needs of these generations.

(Step 4) Indigenous worship celebrations foster worship among all three generations. Musical tastes, teaching styles, and liturgical structure are allowed to become generation specific, while maintaining biblical allegiance and doctrinal fidelity.

(Step 5) Crossing the bridges of God becomes the primary route for the good news to travel. Befriending and multiple invitations emerge as powerful strategies for introducing friends, relatives, associates, and neighbors to the joys of Christian life.

(Step 6) Evaluation becomes our tool for adjusting methodology and tracking progress. Precise evaluation thwarts the natural onset of the "choke law," when existing members begin to absorb the entire time and attention of the church. In addition, a congregation's vital signs are monitored by measuring progress or regress in the four fields of church growth—growing in maturity, growing in unity, growing in favor (among the community), and finally, growing in numbers.

(Step 7) Only when all of the six steps are bathed in the seventh and most important step, prayer, can our plans succeed. A prayer strategy that embraces 50/50 prayer for church members, as well as the unchurched, will release God's hand to work among the church and upon the harvest.

The steps summated above are not intended to encapsulate all that the tri-generational church is, or will become. But, they are a starting place, upon which individual and unique models will rise. Do not think of them as ends in themselves, but as idea generators and abstractions that can guide your congregation into its own distinct tri-generational personality.

New Models Require Creative Thinking

From Augustine to Barth, from Anselm to Kant, and from Bach to Stravinsky, innovative thinkers have one thing in common—they have the ability to think powerfully and flexibly about new models. The tri-generational model requires a rethinking of how the church as organization is managed, and how the church invisible is shepherded. The suggestions put forth by the authors are not immutable edicts, but guidelines and principles that must be indigenized.

Therefore, let your open mind and creative ideas be wed with inter-generational respect—and bathe all in prayer.

NOTES

Preface

1. Margaret Mead, *Culture and Commitment: A Study of the Generation Gap* (Garden City, N.Y.: Doubleday, 1970), p. 62.

Chapter 1: How Generation Gaps Are Tearing Apart Our Churches

1. C. Peter Wagner, *Your Church Can Grow* (Glendale, Calif.: G/L Publications, 1976), pp. 97-109.
2. C. Peter Wagner, *Leading Your Church to Growth* (Glendale, Calif.: G/L Publications, 1984), pp. 73-106.
3. William M. Easum, "Strategic Mapping Is About Breaking New Ground and Learning to Think and Act Differently," *Global Church Growth: Strategies for Today's Leader* (Corunna, Ind.: Church Growth Center, 1995), Vol. XXXII, No. 2, p. 4.
4. United States Bureau of the Census, *Statistical Abstracts of the United States* (Washington, D.C.: Bureau of the Census, 1991).
5. George Barna, *The Barna Report 1994–95: Virtual America* (Ventura, Calif.: G/L Publications, 1994), p. 259, Table 89.
6. The term "unchurched" is used here in lieu of nomenclature such as "born again" or "Christian." Demographers have discovered that these latter terms are often misunderstood by survey respondents and thus, render inaccurate results (*Born Again: A Look at Christians in America.* Ventura: Barna Research Group, 1990, pp. 4-7). In addition, soteriological status with God is a personal relationship, embraced confidentially and individually by our Father with every human. It is thus, understandably, also beyond the researcher's measurement. "Church attendance" is much easier to measure and reveals the extent to which a person is under the influence of Christian discipleship. However, among Christian denominations, and even individual churches within the same denomination, there is a great divergence in the expectations of church attendance. What may seem to some to be an arbitrary line must by necessity be drawn by the authors. Therefore it is presumed that an "unchurched" person is one who attends church only casually and a "churched" person is one who attends church at least twice a month.
7. George Barna, *Virtual America*, pp. 46-48.
8. Loren B. Mead, *Transforming Congregations for the Future* (Bethesda, Md.: The Alban Institute, 1994), p. 128.
9. C. Peter Wagner, *Your Spiritual Gifts Can Help Your Church Grow* (Ventura, Calif.: G/L Publications, 1979), pp. 116-33.
10. Margaret Mead, *Culture and Commitment: A Study of the Generation Gap.* A detailed examination of the anthropological conditions which create generational fissures can be found in Mead's description of three dissimilar forms of culture: postfigurative, cofigurative, and prefigurative. The reader wishing to learn more about the theoretical forces behind generational bias should consult Margaret Mead's engaging book.
11. George Barna, *The Disillusioned Generation: Baby Busters* (Chicago: Northfield, 1994), p. 21.
12. Ibid., p. 18.
13. Ibid., p. 17.
14. C. Peter Wagner, *Your Church Can Grow*, pp. 97-109.
15. Eddie Gibbs, *I Believe in Church Growth* (Grand Rapids, Mich.: Wm. B. Eerdmans, 1981), pp. 276-80.
16. Lyle E. Schaller, *Growing Plans: Strategies to Increase Your Church's Membership* (Nashville: Abingdon, 1983), p. 26.

243

17. Peter Wagner, *Your Church Can Grow*, pp. 101-2. Wagner borrowed the designation "Congregation" for his secondary group from Larry O. Richards, *A New Face for the Church* (Grand Rapids, Mich.: Zondervan, 1970), pp. 34-35. Wagner traditionally has held that this secondary group ranges from 40 to 120 participants, while the smaller cell group contains 3 to 12 people. This methodology creates a missing group of 13 to 39 participants. This may have occurred because the missing segment often vacillates between being a cell and a sub-congregation. However, because the missing group more often exhibits a sub-congregation's fellowship personality, rather than what Wagner (p. 107) calls the cell group's "family" environment, Eddie Gibbs's preference for including Wagner's missing category in the larger sub-congregation is preferred by the authors.
18. Eddie Gibbs, *I Believe in Church Growth*, p. 279.
19. Confusion often arises when categorizing Sunday school classes. Smaller classes will resemble a cell group and demonstrate a measure of intimacy and interpersonal communication. Larger classes will exhibit a sub-congregation's tendency for social activity and individual contribution. Seeking to group all Sunday school classes into one category is ill advised.
20. C. Peter Wagner, *Your Church Can Grow*, pp. 107-8.
21. Lyle E. Schaller, *Effective Church Planning* (Nashville: Abingdon, 1981), pp. 17-63.
22. Lyle E. Schaller, *Growing Plans*, pp. 91-94.
23. George G. Hunter, *The Contagious Congregation* (Nashville: Abingdon Press, 1979), p. 63.
24. Gary L. McIntosh, *One Size Doesn't Fit All: Bringing Out the Best in Any Size Church* (Grand Rapids, Mich.: Fleming H. Revell, 1999), pp. 17-19.
25. Lyle E. Schaller, *The Multiple Staff and the Larger Church* (Nashville: Abingdon, 1980), pp. 27-35.
26. Ibid., p. 31.
27. Ibid.

Chapter 2: The Aftermath of Generational Conflict

1. C. Peter Wagner, *Your Church Can Be Healthy* (Nashville: Abingdon, 1979), pp. 41-50.
2. Ibid., pp. 42-43. Wagner eventually borrowed from Old West idiom the term "ghost town disease" to differentiate old age from the malady the authors call congregational old age.
3. C. Peter Wagner, "Principles and Procedures of Church Growth: American Church Growth," quotation from a lectureship given at Fuller Theological Seminary, Pasadena, Calif.; January 31–February 11, 1983.
4. Walter E. Ziegenhals, *Urban Churches in Transition* (New York: Pilgrim Press, 1978), p. 180.
5. Donald McGavran, *Understanding Church Growth* (Grand Rapids, Mich.: Wm. B. Eerdmans, 1970), p. 22.
6. C. Peter Wagner, *Church Growth and the Whole Gospel: A Biblical Mandate* (San Francisco: Harper & Row, 1981), pp. 53, 54.
7. George Santayana, *The Life of Reason: Or the Phases of Human Progress* (Amherst, N.Y.: Prometheus Books, 1998).
8. Donald McGavran, *Understanding Church Growth*, p. 198.
9. For more on the debate over the "homogeneous unit" principle see C. Peter Wagner, *Your Church Can Grow: Seven Vital Signs of a Healthy Church* (Ventura, Calif.: G/L Publishing, 1976), pp. 110-23; Ralph H. Elliott, *Church Growth That Counts* (Valley Forge, Penn.: Judson Press, 1982), pp. 55-63; and Kent R. Hunter, "What Ever Happened to the Homogeneous Unit Principle?" *Global Church Growth* (Corunna, Ind.: Church Growth Center, 1990), Vol. XXVI, No. 1, pp. 1-4.
10. Information on "seeker sensitive" ministry is available from The Willow Creek Association, P.O. Box 3188, Barrington, IL 60011-3188.

11. Gary L. McIntosh, *Three Generations: Riding the Waves of Change in Your Church* (Grand Rapids, Mich.: Revell, 1995), p. 190.
12. Win Arn and Charles Arn, "Is Your Church Senior Sensitive?" *Global Church Growth: Strategies for Today's Leader* (Corunna, Ind.: Church Growth Center, 1995), Vol. XXXII, No. 3, p.6.
13. Margaret Mead, *Culture and Commitment*, p. 2.
14. Donald A. McGavran and Win Arn, *How to Grow a Church: Conversations About Church Growth* (Glendale, Calif.: G/L Publications, 1973), p. 71.
15. Margaret L. Usdansky, "Rural Areas Are Making a Comeback," *USA TODAY* (Friday, July 15, 1994), p. 8a.
16. Two helpful books on the rural church include Kent R. Hunter's, *The Lord's Harvest and the Rural Church* (Kansas City, Kan.: Beacon Hill Press, 1993), and Edward W. Hassinger, John S. Holik, and J. Kenneth Benson's *The Rural Church: Learning from Three Decades of Change*, Creative Leadership Series, ed. Lyle E. Schaller (Nashville: Abingdon Press, 1988).

Chapter 3: Attitudes That Produce the Gaps

1. George Barna, *The Invisible Generation: Baby Busters* (Glendale, Calif.: Barna Research Group, Ltd., 1992), p. 18.
2. Ibid., pp. 152-54.
3. Ibid., pp. 157-60.
4. John Seabrook, *The New Yorker* (New York: Advance Magazine Publishers, April 25, 1994), pp. 65–66.
5. George Barna, *The Invisible Generation: Baby Busters*, p. 162.
6. Charles Arn, *How to Start a New Service* (Grand Rapids, Mich.: Baker Books, 1997), p. 37.
7. Margaret Mead, *Culture and Commitment: A Study of the Generation Gap*, p. 4.
8. George Barna, *The Invisible Generation: Baby Busters*, p. 157.

Chapter 4: When 1 + 1 + 1 = 1

1. E. Steve Eidson, *When Lines Are Drawn: A Guide to Resolving Conflict in the Church* (Joplin Missouri: College Press, 1994), pp. 85-86.
2. C. Peter Wagner, *Your Spiritual Gifts Can Help Your Church Grow*, p. 260.
3. Margaret Mead, *Culture and Commitment: A Study of the Generation Gap*, p. 2.
4. Lyle E. Schaller, *The Multiple Staff and the Larger Church*, p. 31.
5. C. Peter Wagner, *Leading Your Church to Growth: The Secret of Pastor/People Partnership in Dynamic Church Growth*, p. 212.
6. Lyle Schaller, *The Multiple Staff and the Larger Church*, p. 31.

Chapter 5: Step 1: Envision Your Leadership, Church, and Community

1. Oscar Wilde, letter in *Saint James Gazette* (London, England), 28 June 1890.
2. George Barna, *The Power of Vision: How You Can Capture and Apply God's Vision for Your Ministry* (Ventura, Calif.: Regal Books, 1992), pp. 28, 38-39.
3. Elmer L. Towns, *Vision Day: Capturing the Power of Vision* (Lynchburg, Virginia: Church Growth Institute, 1994), pp. 24-25.
4. George Barna, *The Power of Vision*, pp. 38-39.
5. A philosophy of ministry statement answers the question, "What is the unique personality of your church?" It is also very comprehensive, often reaching several pages in length. The following two books are helpful in discovering and describing your philosophy of ministry. Kent R. Hunter, *Your Church Has*

Personality: Find Your Focus—Maximize Your Mission (Corunna, Ind.: Church Growth Center, 1997) and Harold J. Westing, *Create and Celebrate Your Church's Uniqueness: Designing a Church Philosophy of Ministry* (Grand Rapids, Mich.: Kregel Resources, 1993).
6. Elmer L. Towns, *Vision Day*, pp. 24-26.
7. Elmer Towns' compete and systematic "community survey" can be found in *Vision Day*, appendix.
8. George Barna, *The Power of Vision*, pp. 97-103.
9. Dietrich Bonhoeffer, trans. John W. Doberstein, *Life Together* (New York: Harper and Bros., 1954), p. 81.
10. Ibid., p. 84.
11. C. Peter Wagner, *Leading Your Church to Growth*, p. 168.
12. David Bryant, *Concerts of Prayer; How Christians Can Join Together for Spiritual Awakening and World Evangelism* (Ventura, Calif.: Regal Books, 1988), p. 25.
13. Robert Hargrove, *Masterful Coaching* (San Francisco: Jossey-Bass/Pfeiffer, 1995), p. 176.
14. Leith Anderson, *Dying for Change* (Minneapolis: Bethany Publishing House, 1990), pp. 177-78.
15. Charles Arn, *How to Start a New Service*, pp. 71-76.
16. C. Peter Wagner, *Leading Your Church to Growth*, p. 211.
17. George Barna, *The Power of Vision*, p. 145.

Chapter 6: Step 2: Leading the Tri-generational Church

1. Emil Brunner, trans. Harold Knight, *The Misunderstanding of the Church* (London: Lutterworth Press, 1952), pp. 10, 15-18.
2. David S. Luecke and Samuel Southard, *Pastoral Administration: Integrating Ministry and Management in the Church* (Waco, Texas: Word Books, 1986), pp. 56-57.
3. Kennon L. Callahan, *Twelve Keys to an Effective Church: Strategic Planning for Mission* (San Francisco, Calif.: Harper & Row, Publishers, 1983), p. 60.
4. Ibid., p. 58.
5. "Culture-current" is becoming the preferred term to describe a worship service that is up-to-the minute and incorporates fresh new ideas. Usually these are Gen-X celebrations that combine mixed media formats. Chapter 8 describes these types of celebrations in more detail.
6. Donald A. McGavran, *Effective Evangelism: A Theological Mandate* (Phillipsburg, N.J.: Presbyterian and Reformed Publishing Co., 1988), p. 122.
7. The apostle Paul's model of church planting began with his arrival at the synagogue (Acts 13:14), and followed with an attempt to win his Jewish countrymen (Acts 13:15-41). After gaining a hearing, he often continued with the Gentile God-fearers who were open to his message (Acts 13:46-52). By Acts 17:2, this approach was most likely what is referred to by the expression that Paul ministered "as his custom was."
8. McGavran, *Effective Evangelism*, p 122.
9. Bill and Lynne Hybels, *Rediscovering Church: The Story and Vision of Willow Creek Community Church* (Grand Rapids, Mich.: Zondervan, 1995), p. 185.

Chapter 7: Step 3: Identify the Needs of the Unchurched

1. C. Peter Wagner, *Frontiers in Missionary Strategy* (Chicago: Moody Press, 1971), p. 110.
2. Donald A. McGavran, *Understanding Church Growth*, p. 119.
3. You will find that it often takes more person power to initiate a ministry than to keep it running. The inaugural promotion, start-up, volunteer training and inevitable missteps usually necessitates more assistance and guidance in the earlier stages of program development.
4. Donald A. McGavran, *Understanding Church Growth*, p. 117.

5. David L. Morgan, *Focus Groups As Qualitative Research,* Second ed. (Thousand Oaks, Calif.: Sage, 1977), pp. 35-37.
6. The birth year ranges of the targeted generations are as follows: Generation X, from 1965 to 1983, Boomers, from 1946 to 1964, and for Builders, the year 1945 and before. Birth years are easier to use here than specific ages, since the latter will keep changing. However, use the exact ages in the remainder of this survey.
7. David G. Myers, *Exploring Psychology* (New York: Worth Publishers, 1990), p. 13.
8. The Church Doctor Ministries offers phone research to congregations across the country. They may be reached at 800-869-6444.
9. In most municipalities in the United States, it is against the law to conduct telephone surveys after 9 P.M.

Chapter 8: Step 4: Worship in a Tri-generational Format

1. C. Peter Wagner, *Frontiers in Missionary Strategy,* p. 96.
2. Ibid., p. 97.
3. Elmer L. Towns, *Putting an End to Worship Wars* (Nashville: Broadman & Holman, 1977), p. 136.
4. Charles Arn, *How to Start a New Service,* pp. 91-127, 153-81.
5. Churches that wish to employ multiple worship celebrations to reach different ethnicities should consult the handy volume written by J. Timothy Ahlen and J. V. Thomas titled *One Church, Many Congregations: The Key Church Strategy* (Nashville: Abingdon Press, 1999).
6. Charles Arn, *How to Start a New Service,* pp. 153, 154.
7. Ibid., p. 185.
8. Donald McGavran and George G. Hunter III, *Church Growth Strategies That Work* (Nashville: Abingdon, 1980), p. 34.
9. Elmer L. Towns, *Winning the Winnable* (Lynchburg, Va.: Church Growth Institute, 1987) p. 54.
10. Ibid., p. 43.

Chapter 9: Step 5: Befriending and Inviting

1. Donald A. McGavran, *The Bridges of God* (New York: Friendship Press, 1955).
2. Donald A. McGavran, *Understanding Church Growth,* p. 395.
3. Ibid.
4. George G. Hunter III, *The Contagious Congregation,* pp. 125-26.
5. Donald McGavran and George G. Hunter III, *Church Growth Strategies That Work,* p. 34.
6. Donald A. McGavran, *Understanding Church Growth,* pp. 404-5.
7. George G. Hunter III, *The Contagious Congregation,* p. 119.
8. Elmer L. Towns, *Winning the Winnable,* p. 53.
9. Herb Miller, *How to Build a Magnetic Church* (Nashville: Abingdon, 1987), pp. 36-37.
10. Elmer L. Towns, *Winning the Winnable,* p. 54.
11. The authors are not proposing that it will take exactly seven invitations to elicit a positive response. We do believe it requires multiple tactful invitations, more so than the average person recognizes.

Chapter 10: Step 6: Evaluate Your Success

1. Donald A. McGavran and Winfield C. Arn, *Ten Steps for Church Growth* (New York: Harper & Row, 1977), p. 84.
2. Ibid., p. 85.
3. Donald A. McGavran, *Effective Evangelism,* pp. 48-49.

4. George G. Hunter III, *To Spread the Power: Church Growth in the Wesleyan Spirit* (Nashville: Abingdon, 1987), p. 48.
5. Ibid., p. 46.
6. Donald A. McGavran, *Understanding Church Growth*, p. 93.
7. Ibid., p. 94.
8. C. Peter Wagner, *Frontiers in Missionary Strategy*, p. 22.
9. R. V. G. Tasker, *The Gospel According to St. Matthew: An Introduction and Commentary* (Grand Rapids, Mich.: Eerdmans, 1961), p. 277.
10. Surveys that measure congregational unity tend to produce inflated results, since people usually over-report their level of agreement. Thus, keep in mind this tendency toward inflation when analyzing your results.
11. Typically, a guest can be expected to drive up to twelve and one-half minutes to attend your congregation. However, in metropolitan areas this drive time can increase to 35 minutes. In mountainous terrain and/or areas dotted by small lakes, marshes, and other natural impediments, drive time can drop to 10 minutes or less. Return to chapter 7, if you need to look again at the three steps to computing the distance that potential congregants will drive to your church.
12. Donald A. McGavran, *Understanding Church Growth*, p. 81.
13. Eddie Gibbs, *Body Building Exercises for the Local Church* (London: Falcon, 1979), p. 80.
14. George G. Hunter III, *The Contagious Congregation*, p. 118.

Chapter 11: Step 7: Mobilizing Your Church for Transgenerational Prayer

1. Armin R. Gesswein, "Prayer and Evangelism," in *Evangelism the Next Ten Years*, ed. Sherwood Eliot Wirt (Waco, Texas: Word Books, 1978), p. 97.
2. Elmer L. Towns, *Evangelism and Church Growth: A Practical Encyclopedia* (Ventura, Calif.: Regal Books, 1995), p. 302.
3. Armin R. Gesswein, "Prayer and Evangelism," p. 97.
4. Charles Clark, *Pioneers of Revival* (Plainfield, N.J.: Logos International, 1971), p. 69.
5. Sterling W. Huston, *Crusade Evangelism and the Local Church* (Minneapolis: World Wide Publications, 1984), p. 50.
6. Eddie Gibbs, *I Believe in Church Growth*, p. 188.
7. Ibid.
8. William F. Arndt and F. Wilbur Gingrich, trans. Walter Bauer, *A Greek-English Lexicon of the New Testament and Other Early Christian Literature* (Chicago: University of Chicago Press, 1957), p. 788.
9. David Bryant, *With Concerts of Prayer*, p. 44.
10. Paraphrased by the authors from *Prayer Triplets*, Billy Graham Evangelistic Association (Minneapolis: World Wide Publications).
11. Ibid.
12. Donald A. McGavran, *Understanding Church Growth*, p. 410.
13. Ibid.
14. C. Peter Wagner, *Your Spiritual Gifts Can Help Your Church Grow*, p. 76.
15. Ibid., p. 75.
16. Ibid., p. 76.
17. Terry Teykl, *Making Room to Pray* (Muncie, Ind.: Prayer Point Press, 1993).
18. Terry Teykl, *Blueprint for the House of Prayer* (Muncie, Inds.: Prayer Point Press, 1997), pp. 48-49.

Epilogue: Which Church Will Yours Be in the 21st Century?

1. Margaret Mead, *Culture and Commitment: A Study in the Generation Gap*, p. 2.